COOPERATIVE ENTERPRISES:

KEY DRIVERS IN THE U.S. ECONOMY FROM THE 19TH CENTURY TO TODAY

GETACHEW MERGIA TACHE

AUGUST 2024, SEATTLE, USA

HTTPS://BRIGHTFORCOOPERATIVES.ORG/

CONTENTS

LIST OF FIGURES

ACRONYMS

ACDI/VOCA	Agricultural Cooperative Development International/Volunteers in Overseas Cooperative Assistance
CEPC	Central Electric Power Cooperative in Missouri
CHCA	Cooperative Home Care Associates
CESA	Cooperative Education Services Agency
CES	Cooperative Education Services
GHC-SCW	Group Health Cooperative of South-Central Wisconsin
CHP	Community Health Partners Cooperative
CMERDC	Central Minnesota Educational Research and Development Council
DLDCs	Developing and Least Developed Countries
FCS	Farm Credit System
ILO	International Labour Organization
MCEC	Mid-Carolina Electric Cooperative
MHANY	The Mutual Housing Association of New York
M4P	Market System Development
MOREnet	Missouri Research and Education Network
NCB	National Cooperative Bank
NCBA CLUSA	The National Cooperative Business Association CLUSA
NPGG	North Pacific Grain Growers, Inc.
NRECA	The National Rural Electric Cooperative Association
SACCO	Saving and Credit Cooperative
SERDC	Southwest Educational Development Center
SME	Small and Micro Enterprises
U.S.	United States of America

THE AUTHOR

Getachew Mergia Tache, a specialist in financial inclusion and Cooperative-based community economic development. Holding a spectrum of professional certifications, including Market System Development (M4P), Rural Finance, Value Chain Finance, Agricultural Goods Lease Financing, SME Finance, and Microfinance, he stands as a recognized expert. The Ethiopian Management Institute has qualified him professionally as a consultant specializing in Cooperatives, Financial Cooperatives, and Community-based Economic Development.

Getachew's expertise is a result of comprehensive training in promoting and managing cooperative enterprises and community-based economic development, courtesy of Mekelle University and Makerere University. Armed with a BSc in Agriculture (1994) and an MA Degree in Cooperative Marketing (2010), he boasts over 25 years of rich experience that spans both the private and public sectors.

Notably, Getachew underwent on-the-job training as a Rural SACCO promotion and management expert facilitated by ACDI/VOCA from Jan 1, 2001, to Dec 31, 2003. Additionally, he successfully completed a certified Microfinance Expert program facilitated by the Frankfurt School of Finance and Management. His commitment to continuous learning led him to the Market System Development-Making Market Work for the Poor (M4P) Training held at the Springfield Development Centre in Bangkok, Thailand, Cooperative Business Management and Financing in The Co-operative University of Kenya and The Institute of Co-operative Management, Pune India.

With a wealth of experience, Getachew has played diverse roles in Financial Inclusion, Rural Finance, SME Finance, Agricultural Value Chain Finance, and Cooperative Development. His contributions have left an indelible mark in both Ethiopia and Uganda.

ABSTRACT

This paper reviews the significant role of the cooperative movement in various sectors of the U.S. economy, emphasizing its impact on empowering farmers, consumers, and workers through resource pooling, cost reduction, and control over supply chains and market prices. Cooperative enterprises have grown beyond their agricultural origins to become influential across diverse sectors, significantly shaping the U.S. economy throughout history. They have been crucial in enhancing living standards, fostering job creation, and driving modernization. This paper examines their importance across key economic periods:

1. 19th Century (Late 1800s): The cooperative movement gained momentum in the late 1800s. Organizations like the Grange (established in 1867) and the Farmers' Alliance (founded in the 1870s) helped farmers pool resources, reduce costs, and gain more control over supply chains and market prices (Hoyt, 1951).

2. Early 20th Century: The early 1900s saw continued growth of the cooperative movement. Agricultural cooperatives provided crucial support to farmers during economic hardships by reducing costs through collective purchasing, marketing, and credit access (Birchall, 2012).

3. Great Depression (1930s): The Great Depression significantly boosted cooperative activities as people sought ways to cope with the economic downturn. Credit unions, consumer cooperatives, and rural electric cooperatives emerged during this period. New Deal policies under Roosevelt supported these initiatives, recognizing the potential of cooperatives in economic recovery (Roosevelt, 1938).

4. Post-World War II Era: After World War II, cooperatives continued to play a vital role, especially in rural areas. They contributed to the modernization of agriculture, expanded access to electricity, and improved living standards. This period also saw

saw the growth of housing and worker cooperatives (Deller et al., 2017).

5. Today's U.S. Economy: Cooperative enterprises remain significant in the modern U.S. economy. They are crucial in rural areas for modernizing agriculture, expanding electricity access, improving living standards, and providing financial services through credit unions and mutual insurance. Additionally, cooperatives create employment in both rural and urban settings (Gordon Nembhard, 2014).

This paper highlights how cooperative enterprises have evolved from their agricultural roots to become pivotal in various U.S. economic sectors, including agriculture and agro-processing, manufacturing, finance and insurance, housing, retail, and utilities. Their role in promoting economic resilience, fostering community development, and enhancing job quality underscores their enduring significance in U.S. economic history and contemporary society (Adams, 2013).

I. Introduction

BRIEF INTRODUCTION TO COOPERATIVE ENTERPRISES

Cooperative enterprises, commonly referred to as cooperatives or co-ops, are businesses owned and operated by a group of individuals, the members, for their mutual benefit. Unlike traditional businesses that prioritize profit maximization for shareholders, cooperatives prioritize the needs and interests of their members, who are also their owners. This model is grounded in the principles of democratic control, economic participation, and shared ownership and value of not-for-profit-driven business practices (Birchall, 2012).

Cooperatives come in various forms and serve diverse purposes, including agricultural cooperatives, credit unions, consumer cooperatives, housing cooperatives, and worker cooperatives. Each type addresses the specific needs of its members, ranging from pooling resources and reducing costs to accessing credit and securing housing (Hoyt, 1951).

To understand how cooperative enterprises have evolved and adapted to meet the economic and social needs of their members and the surrounding communities over time, it is important to illustrate the foundational principles of cooperatives: democratic ownership, equitable benefit distribution, and community-focused initiatives.

For instance, the Rochdale Society of Equitable Pioneers, founded in 1844 in England, serves as a pioneering example of the cooperative movement. It aimed to provide affordable, high-quality food to members who faced exploitative conditions during the Industrial Revolution. This cooperative model emphasized democratic governance and equitable distribution of benefits among members, marking a departure from the profit-driven business practices of the time (Fairbairn, 1994).

EXPLANATION OF THEIR MEMBER-OWNED BUSINESS MODEL

The cooperative business model is distinguished by its emphasis on member ownership and democratic governance. In a cooperative, each member typically has one vote, regardless of the amount of capital they have invested. This ensures that all members have an equal say in decision-making processes, fostering a sense of ownership, shared responsibility, and accountability (Birchall, 2012).

Members contribute investment capital and democratically make decisions on how and where to invest and control the capital of their cooperative. Surplus earnings are either reinvested in the cooperative or distributed among members based on their usage of the cooperative's services (patronage), rather than on the capital they have invested. This model promotes economic fairness and ensures that the benefits of the cooperative are directly tied to the members' economic involvement and needs (International Co-operative Alliance, 2020).

A concrete example is the Mondragon Cooperative in Spain, founded in 1956. The Mondragon Cooperative is one of the world's largest and most successful worker cooperatives, operating various businesses including manufacturing, finance, and retail, all owned and governed by its worker-members. Decisions are made democratically, and profits are shared among members, contributing to job security and community development (Cheney, 1999).

The Mondragon Cooperative demonstrates the cooperative model's adaptability across different sectors and its potential to foster inclusive economic development. It clearly shows how cooperative principles of democratic governance and equitable profit-sharing can lead to sustainable economic growth and member well-being (Whyte & Whyte, 1991).

While the Mondragon Cooperative is one of the most famous worker cooperative examples globally, the United States also has several notable worker cooperatives that operate successfully.

1. Equal Exchange: Formed in 1986 in Massachusetts, Equal Exchange is a worker cooperative that focuses on fair trade products, primarily distributing organic, gourmet coffee, tea, sugar, bananas, avocados, cocoa, and chocolate bars produced by farmer cooperatives in Latin America, Africa, and Asia[]. It operates on democratic principles where employees are also owners of the company (Equal Exchange, n.d.).

2. Evergreen Cooperatives: Located in Cleveland, Ohio, Evergreen Cooperatives set out in 2008 with a strategic vision focused on economic inclusion and building the local economy by creating green jobs[]. It is a network of worker-owned businesses that includes a laundry service, a solar energy company, and an urban agriculture initiative, all aimed at creating jobs and building wealth in low-income neighborhoods (Alperovitz et al., 2011).

3. Isthmus Engineering and Manufacturing: Located in Madison, Wisconsin, Isthmus Engineering is a worker cooperative specializing in the precision design and manufacture of custom automation machinery[]. Established in 1980 as a partnership and becoming a worker cooperative in 1983, it offers services such as robotic integration and system integration to various industries, including automotive, consumer products, medical, industrial, and solar. About half of its members are engineers, and the other half are electricians, machinists, and mechanics (Isthmus Engineering, n.d.).

4. A Slice of New York: A worker cooperative pizzeria in San Jose, California, became an employee-owned cooperative in 2017 with the goal of providing stability and growth opportunities for its worker-members[] (A Slice of New York, n.d.).

5. Mujeres Unidas: A worker cooperative in Chicago, Illinois, that provides domestic cleaning services. Owned and operated by its members, Mujeres Unidas operates as a non-profit organization known by the name "Women Together," established in 1978 to support victims of family violence and survivors of sexual assault and their families. It provides shelter to live in and supports the

victims and survivors of sexual assault with appropriate services (Mujeres Unidas, n.d.).

These examples demonstrate the diversity of worker cooperatives in the U.S. across different sectors, showing how they operate democratically and provide economic benefits and job security to their members.

HISTORICAL OVERVIEW OF COOPERATIVES, ONGOING SIGNIFICANCE IN THE U.S. ECONOMY

Cooperatives have been a vital part of the U.S. economy for over a century, adapting to meet the changing needs of their members and communities. Their historical significance is rooted in their ability to provide economic stability and self-reliance during challenging times (Hoyt, 1951).

In the late 1800s, farmers in the United States began forming cooperatives to pool resources, reduce costs, and gain greater control over market prices. This early cooperative movement helped to mitigate the economic challenges faced by rural communities and laid the foundation for future cooperative development (Hoyt, 1951).

The Great Depression of the 1930s marked a period of significant growth for cooperatives, as many people turned to this model to survive economic hardship. Credit unions, consumer cooperatives, and rural electric cooperatives emerged, supported by New Deal policies that recognized the potential of cooperatives to aid in economic recovery (Roosevelt, 1938).

After World War II, cooperatives continued to play a crucial role in modernizing agriculture, expanding access to electricity, and improving living standards, particularly in rural areas. The cooperative model also saw growth in urban areas, with the establishment of housing cooperatives and worker cooperatives (Birchall, 2012).

Example:

During the Great Depression, the Tennessee Valley Authority (TVA) in the U.S. supported the formation of rural electric cooperatives to bring electricity to underserved rural areas. This initiative not only improved living standards but also stimulated economic development by enabling agricultural modernization and rural industry growth (Adams, 2013). TVA demonstrates how cooperative enterprises can play a role in addressing critical infrastructure gaps and contribute to regional economic development if supported by government initiatives such as appropriate support functions and rules. It underscores the historical role of cooperatives in providing essential services and fostering community resilience during economic crises (Cronon, 1991).

Today, cooperatives remain significant in the U.S. economy, continuing to enhance living standards, modernize agriculture, and expand access to essential services such as electricity, housing, and finance. They foster economic self-reliance and community development, proving to be resilient and adaptable across various economic sectors (Deller et al., 2017).

Example: Credit Unions

During the Great Depression, traditional banks were reluctant to lend, particularly to lower-income individuals and rural communities. Credit unions stepped in to fill this gap, offering much-needed access to credit. Credit unions have played a vital role in providing financial services to underserved communities during the Great Depression and continue to do so today in the U.S. financial market (Greenberg, 1986). Their cooperative structure, community focus, and commitment to financial inclusion and education distinguish them from traditional banks, making them a crucial component of the U.S. financial system. By understanding and leveraging the strengths of credit unions, policymakers and community leaders designed appropriate support functions and rules to promote them for economic empowerment and resilience in diverse communities across the United States (NCUA, 2024).

According to NCUA Chairman Todd M. Harper, as of March 31, 2024, there are more than 4,500 federally insured credit unions in the U.S., serving over 140 million members and holding assets of $2.31 trillion[5]. These institutions play a crucial role in enhancing financial inclusion and economic empowerment (NCUA, 2024).

U.S. Credit Unions differ from the traditional banking system for several key reasons:

- Member Ownership and Democratic Governance: Credit unions operate under a cooperative model where members are owners and have democratic control. Each member has an equal say in decision-making processes, ensuring that the institution operates in the best interests of its members and the local community (Birchall, 2012).
- Community Impact: Credit Unions are known for their community-focused approach, providing personalized financial services tailored to the needs of their members. They often serve underserved populations and geographic areas where access to traditional banking services may be limited (Gordon Nembhard, 2014).
- Economic Empowerment: By offering affordable financial products and services, credit unions contribute to economic empowerment. They help individuals and families build savings, access credit for major purchases or emergencies, and achieve financial goals (NCUA, 2024).
- Resilience and Stability: During economic downturns and financial crises, credit unions have historically demonstrated resilience and stability in the U.S. financial market. Their cooperative structure and conservative financial practices prioritize member interests and long-term sustainability (Greenberg, 1986).
- Promotion of Financial Health: Through financial education programs and counseling services, credit unions promote financial literacy and empower members to make informed financial decisions, thereby improving overall financial health and well-being (Deller et al., 2017).

This example illustrates how credit unions, as a form of cooperative enterprise, remain significant in the U.S. economy by promoting financial inclusivity, community development, and economic resilience. They provide communities with alternatives to traditional financial services and exemplify the cooperative principles of member ownership, democratic governance, and shared economic benefits, demonstrating their enduring relevance and impact in modern economic landscapes (NCUA, 2024). In conclusion, credit unions exemplify the enduring significance of cooperative enterprises in the U.S. economy.

II. 19th Century (Late 1800s)

ORIGINS OF THE COOPERATIVE MOVEMENT IN THE U.S.

The cooperative movement in the United States began in the late 19th century as a response to the economic challenges faced by farmers and rural communities. The Industrial Revolution brought significant changes to agriculture, including the mechanization of farming and the rise of agribusiness. These changes led to increased unfair competition and market domination by a few, lower crop prices, and higher costs for supplies and equipment. Farmers and rural communities, often isolated in rural areas and lacking bargaining power, struggled to compete in the evolving market (Adams, 2013).

The cooperative movement emerged as a grassroots response to these challenges, inspired by similar movements in Europe, particularly the Rochdale Pioneers in England. The principles of cooperation —democratic control, shared ownership, and economic participation resonated with American farmers who sought to regain control over their economic destinies (Hoyt, 1951).

ESTABLISHMENT OF FARMERS' COOPERATIVES

Two key organizations were instrumental in the establishment of farmers' cooperatives in the United States during the late 1800s: the Grange and the Farmers' Alliance.

- **The Grange (founded in 1867)**

The Grange, also known as The National Grange of the Order of Patrons of Husbandry, was the first successful national farming organization, founded in 1867 by Oliver Hudson Kelley. The Grange aimed to address the social and economic needs of farmers by promoting cooperative principles and practices. It encouraged farmers to come together to pool resources, share knowledge, and advocate for their interests. The Grange established cooperative stores, grain elevators, and other businesses to help farmers reduce costs and improve their economic position. By working collectively, Grange members were able to negotiate better prices for supplies and secure fairer market conditions for their products (Cronon, 1991). The National Grange still exists today with 2,000 local community Granges across 41 states and nearly 80,000 members[6]. The organization is actively involved in various community and agricultural initiatives, supporting economic development and fostering community resilience (National Grange, 2023).

- **Farmers' Alliance (founded in the 1870s)**

The Farmers' Alliance, founded in the 1870s, was a crucial organization in the cooperative movement. Divided into the Southern Alliance and the Northwestern Alliance, it aimed to improve farmers' economic conditions through education, economic cooperation, and political advocacy. The Alliance established cooperative buying and selling organizations to help farmers purchase supplies at lower prices and sell products at fairer rates. They also pushed for political reforms, such as regulating railroad rates and creating a sub-treasury system for low-interest loans (Gordon Nembhard, 2014).

However, the Alliance failed as a cooperative economic movement because it shifted into a political movement, evolving into the Populist Political Party in 1892. This transformation underscores the importance of cooperative leadership and members maintaining control over their mission to avoid mission drift. Otherwise, their cooperative will lose its original purpose and effectiveness (Hoyt, 1951).

Organizations like The Grange and the Farmers' Alliance played crucial roles in advocating for cooperative principles and establishing cooperative businesses. These early cooperatives laid the groundwork for the ongoing growth and significance of the cooperative model in the U.S. economy, empowering farmers economically and enhancing their social cohesion within rural communities (Adams, 2013).

ROLE OF COOPERATIVE ENTERPRISES IN EMPOWERING US FARMERS

The cooperative model enabled farmers to pool their resources, which was essential for reducing individual costs and gaining greater market leverage. By combining their purchasing power, farmers could buy supplies in bulk at discounted prices combined with after-sales services, this contributes to better use, lowering their overall expenses and brings overall members income and business success (Hoyt, 1951). Similarly, by selling their output products collectively, they could negotiate better prices and terms, thus stabilizing their incomes (Gordon Nembhard, 2014).

Cooperatives also provided farmers with access to essential services and infrastructure that they could not afford individually. For example, cooperative grain elevators allowed farmers to store their grain until market conditions were favorable, rather than being forced to sell at low prices immediately after harvest. These grain elevator, provide a vital service by enabling farmers to leverage their stored grain to access much-needed financing, enhancing their financial stability, since Farmers can use the grain elevator store receipts as collateral to obtain loans from banks or other lending institutions (Cronon, 1991). Cooperative stores offered a range of goods at lower prices than commercial retailers, further reducing costs for members (Adams, 2013). They also helped farmers establish processing facilities for better prices and longer shelf life of products.

Moreover, cooperatives fostered a sense of community and mutual support among farmers. By working together, they could share knowledge, techniques, and innovations, improving their farming practices and productivity. This collaborative spirit helped to build resilient rural communities that could better withstand economic challenges (National Grange, 2023).

Example: Cooperative Grain Elevators

Cooperative grain elevators were a response to the economic challenges faced by farmers due to the mechanization of agriculture, transportation advancements, and the increasing consolidation of markets by large corporations. During the late 19th and early 20th centuries, farmers encountered significant difficulties in storing and marketing their grain effectively. Individual farmers often lacked the capacity to store their harvests beyond immediate needs and were vulnerable to volatile market prices. Cooperative grain elevators emerged as a solution to these challenges (Adams, 2013):

1. Pooling Resources: Farmers in a region would come together to form a cooperative grain elevator. Each member contributed financially to build and maintain the elevator infrastructure, which included storage bins and handling equipment. This pooling of resources allowed farmers to collectively invest in facilities that none could afford individually (Hoyt, 1951).

2. Reducing Costs: By sharing the costs of infrastructure and operations, cooperative grain elevators lowered the per-unit cost of storing grain. This was crucial for farmers who needed to store their grain post-harvest to await better market conditions. Instead of selling at lower prices immediately after harvest, farmers could store their grain in the cooperative elevator and wait for better market opportunities, thereby maximizing their returns. The grain elevator stores issued receipts to the farmers, which could be used as collateral to obtain loans from banks or other lending Institutions lending institutions (Cronon, 1991).

3. Controlling Market Prices: Cooperative grain elevators gave farmers greater bargaining power in the market. By consolidating their grain supplies, cooperatives could negotiate better prices with buyers such as grain merchants and mills. This collective approach enabled farmers to achieve more favorable terms than they could have obtained individually, thus helping to stabilize

and sometimes even influence local market prices (Gordon Nemb-hard, 2014).

4. Community Benefits: Beyond economic benefits, cooperative grain elevators fostered community solidarity and knowledge-sharing among farmers. They provided a forum for farmers to exchange information on best practices in farming, grain storage techniques, and market conditions. This collaborative environment enhanced the overall agricultural productivity of the region (National Grange, 2023)

Figure 1: Enormous Farmers Co-Op grain elevator outside Ogden, Utah

Source : https://www.loc.gov/item/2023697728

In summary, cooperative grain elevators exemplify the transformative power of cooperatives in enabling farmers to pool resources, reduce costs, access finance, and exert greater control over market prices. By working together through cooperatives, farmers could mitigate economic risks, enhance their bargaining power, gain fair market prices for their output, and strengthen their communities economically and socially.

Cooperative grain elevators emerged primarily in agricultural regions across the United States during the late 19th and early 20th centuries. Here's how and where cooperative grain elevators emerged:

1. **Midwestern and Great Plains States:**

• Promotion of Financial Health: Through financial education programs and counseling services, credit unions promote financial literacy and empower members to make informed financial decisions, thereby improving overall financial health and well-being (Deller et al., 2017).Cooperative grain elevators emerged prominently in states such as Iowa, Kansas, Nebraska, and Minnesota. These regions, major grain-producing areas, had fertile lands suitable for growing grains like corn, wheat, and soybeans (Hoyt, 1951).

• The need for cooperative grain storage and marketing facilities was particularly acute due to the large volumes of grain produced and the long distances to major markets.

2. **Rural Communities:**

• Typically, Cooperative grain elevators were established in rural communities where farmers lived and worked. These areas often lacked private grain storage facilities or faced monopolistic practices from commercial grain buyers and storage operators.

• Farmers banded together to form cooperatives, pooling their resources to build grain elevators serving their collective interests (Adams, 2013).

3. **Emergence and Spread:**

• The cooperative grain elevator movement was influenced by the broader cooperative movement in the late 19th century, inspired by European cooperative principles and practices, particularly those of the Rochdale Pioneers.

• Organizations like The Grange and the Farmers' Alliance, which promoted cooperative ideals among farmers, played a significant role in encouraging the establishment of cooperative grain elevators by promoting cooperative ideals among farmers (National Grange, 2023; Gordon Nembhard, 2014). Initially, cooperative grain elevators were grassroots initiatives, often started by local farmers recognizing the benefits of collective action, in dealing with the challenges of storing and marketing grain.

4. **Government Support:**

• During the Great Depression era and later under New Deal policies, the federal government supported the establishment and operation of cooperative enterprises, including grain elevators.
• Rural development and agricultural assistance Programs encouraged the formation of cooperatives as a means to improve the economic conditions of farmers and rural communities (Cronon, 1991).

Summary Points

• Pool Resources: Farmers united to share costs and resources needed for grain storage and marketing infrastructure.
• Reduce Costs: Consolidation through cooperatives lowered individual storage and transportation costs.
• Access Finance: Cooperative grain elevators provided collateral (storage receipts) for loans, aiding cash flow management and investment (Deller et al., 2017).
• Control Market Prices: Collective marketing of grain provided farmers with leverage against monopolistic practices and achieved fairer prices for their produce.

In essence, cooperative grain elevators were a grassroots response to economic pressures faced by farmers, including market fluctuations, transportation costs, limited finance access, and monopolistic practices. This cooperative approach not only addressed immediate economic challenges but also fostered long-term resilience and community cohesion in agricultural regions across the United States.

III. Early 20th Century

GROWTH OF THE COOPERATIVE MOVEMENT IN THE EARLY 1900S

The early 20th century was a pivotal period for the cooperative movement in the United States, marked by significant growth and adaptation in response to rapid industrialization, urbanization, and economic fluctuations. As the country transitioned from an agrarian to an industrial economy, cooperatives emerged as crucial mechanisms for economic stability and community development, especially in agriculture. The following highlights the key aspects of this transformative period:

1. Rapid Industrialization and Urbanization

- Economic Transition: The shift from an agrarian to an industrial economy led to profound changes in how goods were produced, distributed, and consumed. Industrialization brought about new technologies and processes that transformed agriculture and other sectors.
- Urbanization: As people migrated to urban areas in search of industrial jobs, rural communities faced challenges such as reduced labor availability and increased economic pressures. Cooperatives played a vital role in supporting farmers and rural areas during this period of change (Cronon, 1991).

2. Expansion of Cooperatives

- Agricultural Cooperatives: Cooperatives became essential for farmers facing economic volatility and market challenges. They provided mechanisms for pooling resources, accessing larger markets, and negotiating better prices (Deller et al., 2017).

- Other Sectors: Beyond agriculture, cooperatives also began to expand into other areas, including housing, retail, and credit unions, offering new avenues for economic stability and community development (Kawano, 2013).

3. Challenges Faced

- Economic Fluctuations: The early 20th century was marked by economic instability, including periods of recession and financial crises. Cooperatives had to navigate these fluctuations while striving to maintain stability and growth (Adams, 2013).
- Competitive Pressures: Cooperatives often competed with large, well-funded corporations that had significant market power. This competition challenged cooperatives to innovate and improve their operations to stay competitive (Greenberg, 1986).

4. Opportunities and Impact

- Community Solidarity: The cooperative model resonated with those seeking community-based solutions and democratic decision-making processes. Cooperatives fostered a sense of solidarity and mutual support among members (Deller et al., 2017).
- Economic Stability: By pooling resources and leveraging collective bargaining, cooperatives provided members with financial stability and access to better market opportunities. They helped farmers and other producers manage risks and improve their economic conditions (Gordon Nembhard, 2014).

5. Adaptation and Growth

- Education and Training: Cooperatives invested in educating members about cooperative principles and management practices. This investment helped members effectively participate in and manage their cooperatives (Shaffer, 2006).

● Legal and Policy Advocacy: Cooperatives lobbied for legislative reforms and policies that supported their unique organizational structures and addressed barriers to their growth (Hoyt, 1951).

Summary

The early 20th century was a transformative period for the cooperative movement in the United States. Cooperatives adapted to the challenges of industrialization, urbanization, and economic instability, emerging as crucial mechanisms for economic stability and community development. Their growth and success during this period laid the foundation for their continued relevance in American economic and social life.

Despite these challenges, cooperatives persisted and played a crucial role in providing economic stability, community development, and empowerment for their members. Overcoming these obstacles required advocacy for legislative reforms, educational initiatives to promote cooperative principles, and strategic alliances to enhance market access and competitiveness. The cooperative movement continued to evolve, adapting to changing economic conditions and societal needs, and laid the groundwork for its enduring impact on American agriculture and community development.

Opportunities for the Cooperative Model:

1. Community Support and Solidarity: The cooperative model appealed to individuals seeking community-based solutions that emphasized democratic decision-making and shared economic benefits.

2. Access to Markets: Cooperatives provided small farmers and producers with collective market access, enabling them to negotiate better prices and access broader markets than they could individually.

3. Financial Stability: By pooling resources and leveraging economies of scale, cooperatives offered members financial stability, access to credit through collective collateral (such as pooled pooled assets or stored product receipts), and better terms for loans.

4. Social Advocacy: Cooperatives advocated for fairer economic practices and policies that supported small farmers and workers, gaining support from policymakers and the public.

Overall, these opportunities allowed cooperatives to not only survive but also thrive in a competitive economic environment. By emphasizing community solidarity, accessing markets collectively, ensuring financial stability, and advocating for social and economic fairness, cooperatives contributed significantly to the empowerment and economic resilience of their members during this transformative period in American history.

OVERCOMING CHALLENGES AND UTILIZING OPPORTUNITIES:

1. Education and Training: Cooperatives invested in educating members about cooperative principles, management, and market strategies, empowering them to manage and participate effectively (Shaffer, 2006). This empowered members to effectively participate in and manage their cooperative enterprises.

2. Legal Advocacy: Cooperatives lobbied for legislative changes that recognized and supported their unique structures and economic contributions, including fair competition laws (Hoyt, 1951). This included advocating for fair competition laws and regulations that leveled the playing field against larger corporations.

3. Diversification and Innovation: Cooperatives diversified their services and products, embraced technological innovations, and adapted to market changes to improve efficiency and competitiveness (Gordon Nembhard, 2014).

4. Networking and Collaboration: Cooperatives formed networks and alliances to share resources, knowledge, and best practices, enhancing their collective bargaining power and resilience (Kawano, 2013). This local and national collaboration not only help cooperatives to share best practices but also strengthened their collective bargaining power and resilience against economic pressures.

Through these strategic initiatives, cooperatives not only addressed internal challenges but also capitalized on external opportunities to strengthen their economic impact, promote community development, and advocate for fairer economic practices. This proactive approach contributed to the enduring relevance and success of the cooperative model in American agriculture and beyond.

Investing to Overcome Challenges and Utilize Opportunities

During the early 20th century in the United States, the cooperative movement faced significant challenges in securing financing for various initiatives. However, by employing strategic approaches to overcome the financial challenges not only support their operational needs but also enhanced their ability to effectively serve members and advocate for better enabling environment. Cooperatives typically designed a proactive strategy to obtain finance to invest for member education, lobby for legislative changes, and pursue other initiatives through several key sources:

1. Member Investments and Contributions: Members contributed financially through fees, share purchases, or equity investments to support education and other initiatives (Deller et al., 2017). These

Member contributed funds where instrumental to support educational programs, training workshops, and other member-focused initiatives.

2. Retained Earnings: Cooperatives retained some portion of its profits to reinvest in various initiatives such as educational activities, infrastructure, and advocacy efforts (Greenberg, 1986).

3. Loans and Credit Facilities: cooperatives access loans and credit from supportive financial institutions, including cooperative banks and credit unions that understand and support cooperative enterprises' business. Mostly they use these funds for capital investments, project expansion, and operational needs (Adams, 2013).

4. Grants and Donations: Cooperatives sought grants and donations from government agencies, foundations, and private donors to support development and advocacy initiatives (Gordon Nembhard, 2014).

5. Cooperative Development Funds: Some cooperatives benefit from cooperative development funds provided by government programs or cooperative associations (Kawano, 2013). These funds are specifically designed to support cooperative enterprises in their development, growth, and sustainability efforts.

6. Income from Services: Cooperatives generate income from services to reinvest into educational programs and advocacy and useful projects. This is supported by studies on how cooperatives used generated income (Shaffer, 2006).

7. Mutual Support and Collaboration: Cooperatives collaborated with other cooperatives and community organizations to pool resources and extend funding opportunities, as well as share costs, and leverage funding opportunities for mutual benefit (Cronon, 1991), This collaborative approach extends the reach and impact of financial resources available to cooperatives.

In Summary, during a challenging economic and regulatory environment, cooperatives utilized a variety of financial strategies to invest in education, advocacy, and other initiatives crucial for their members' welfare and community impact. These efforts helped strengthen their resilience and effectiveness in achieving their cooperative goals at all times of economic hardship.

Benefits for Members:

- Economic Empowerment: Members of cooperatives enjoyed from stable prices, fairer wages, and access to markets and financial services that enhanced their economic well-being (Deller et al., 2017).
- Social Cohesion: Cooperatives promoted community solidarity and cohesion by promoting mutual support, democratic governance, and shared prosperity among members (Kawano, 2013).
- Sustainability: Cooperatives contributed to long-term environmental and economic sustainability through sustainable practices and local economic development in their communities (Greenberg, 1986).

In summary, during the early 20th century, the cooperative movement in the United States navigated challenges such as economic instability and competitive pressures while leveraging opportunities like community support and market access. Through education, advocacy, innovation, and collaboration, cooperatives overcame these challenges to benefit their members economically, socially, and environmentally, thereby solidifying their role as effective models for community development and economic resilience.

FORMATION AND IMPACT OF AGRICULTURAL COOPERATIVES

Agricultural cooperatives played a crucial role in supporting farmers during the early 20th century. These cooperatives were formed to address the economic challenges that farmers faced, including fluctuating crop prices, high input costs, and limited access to credit. By coming together, farmers were able to leverage their collective strength to improve their economic conditions.

One significant example of agricultural cooperatives' impact was the formation of marketing cooperatives. These cooperatives allowed farmers to collectively market their products, which helped stabilize prices and ensured that farmers received a fair return for their produce. Marketing cooperatives also enabled farmers to reach broader markets and negotiate better terms with buyers (Adams, 2013).

In addition to marketing cooperatives, supply cooperatives were established to help farmers purchase inputs such as seeds, fertilizers, and equipment at lower costs. By buying in bulk, supply cooperatives were able to secure discounts from suppliers, reducing the overall expenses for individual farmers (Hoyt, 1951).

Examples of U.S. Agricultural Cooperatives

1. Agricultural Marketing Cooperatives: Sunkist Growers, Inc.

- Overview: Founded in 1893, Sunkist Growers, Inc. is one of the most prominent marketing cooperatives in the United States. It is a cooperative of citrus growers based primarily in California and Arizona.
- Impact: Sunkist has successfully provided its members with a collective marketing platform, helping to stabilize prices and ensure that farmers receive fair returns for their citrus products. The cooperative's brand is recognized globally, which helps its

members access broader markets and negotiate better terms with buyers.

Figure 2: Products of Sunkist Growers, Inc

Source: https://www.sunkist.com

• Today, the status ofSunkist Growers, Inc as one of big Agricultural Marketing Cooperatives

• Sunkist Growers remains a significant player in the citrus industry, maintaining a strong market share in the U.S. and internationally. They are recognized as the largest fresh produce citrus marketing cooperative in the world with robust financial position.

• Sunkist employs around 1,000 people directly and supports numerous jobs indirectly through its network of member growers and associated businesses

2. Agricultural Supply Cooperatives:

• CHS Inc. established in 1929 by North Pacific Grain Growers, Inc. (NPGG) is organized as a regional cooperative, with 60 affiliated local cooperatives. CHS Inc., is based in the United States, with headquarters near St. Paul, Minnesota, and has office in Calgary, Alberta,Canada. originally known as Cenex Harvest States Cooperatives, is one of the largest supply cooperatives in the U.S. It provides a wide range of agricultural inputs, including fuels, fertilisers, seeds, and crop protection products.

• Impact: By purchasing inputs in bulk, CHS Inc. secures discounts from suppliers, which are then passed on to member farmers. This reduces overall expenses for individual farmers, helping to improve their profitability and sustainability.

Figure 3: Facilities of CHS, Inc

Source: https://www.chsinc.com/

Today, the status of as one of the big Agricultural Supply Cooperatives

• CHS Inc. is the largest agricultural supply cooperative in the U.S. with annual revenues exceeding $47 billion as of 2023. It holds a substantial share in the agribusiness sector, dealing with energy, grains, and food production.

The cooperative's total assets are valued at approximately $18.6 billion. This includes extensive infrastructure, such as grain elevators, refineries, and other facilities critical to its operations. CHS also owns petroleum refineries, processing plants, grain terminals, crop protection and crop nutrients facilities, and ag retail business units across the U.S. to provide its owners with a direct link, to where they live and work, from planting to harvest to consumers.

• CHS Inc. employs over 10,000 people globally, with a significant number based in the U.S., supporting its diverse range of agribusiness operations.

3. Combination Type of Agricultural Supply and Marketing Cooperatives:
Land O'Lakes, Inc.

● Land O'Lakes, Inc., established in 1921, operates both as a supply and marketing cooperative. It is one of America's premier agribusiness and food member-owned cooperative companies. It serves dairy farmers by providing them with animal feed, seed, and other agricultural supplies, and also markets their dairy products.

● Impact: By combining supply and marketing functions, Land O'Lakes offers a comprehensive suite of services to its members. This integration helps reduce costs for farmers, improve product quality, and ensure better market access and price stability for dairy products. The cooperative's strong brand presence in the dairy market also aids in securing favorable terms for its members.

● Today, the status of as one of the biggest Agricultural Supply and Marketing Cooperatives Lis notable. LandO'Lakes, Inc. is a leading agribusiness and food cooperative with 2023 annual sales totaling $17 billion. It is ranked 213 on the Fortune 500 list, indicating its significant market presence.

● Land O'Lakes' total assets are substantial, including properties and facilities across agricultural production, consumer foods, and other sectors.

The cooperative employs over 10,000 people, contributing to a wide range of operations from agricultural inputs to food production.

These examples illustrate how agricultural cooperatives in the U.S. have successfully supported farmers by leveraging collective strength to stabilize prices, reduce costs, and improve market access. These cooperatives play vital roles in their respective industries, providing significant employment opportunities and maintaining strong financial positions to support their member-owners and communities (Birchall, 2012).

SUPPORT FOR FARMERS DURING ECONOMIC HARDSHIPS

The early 20th century was also a period of economic hardship for many farmers, exacerbated by events such as the Dust Bowl and the Great Depression. During these challenging times, cooperatives provided critical support to farmers, helping them to survive and even thrive despite adverse conditions.

During the Great Depression farmers struggled with falling crop prices and rising debt. Agricultural cooperatives provided a lifeline by offering lower-cost supplies, better marketing opportunities, and access to credit. The cooperative model allowed farmers to band together and support one another, creating a buffer against the worst effects of the economic downturn.

1. Purchasing Supplies: Cooperative supply associations emerged as an essential organization for farmers struggling to afford essential inputs such as seeds, fertilizers, and equipment. By pooling their purchasing power, farmers could buy in bulk directly from suppliers and directly from manufacturers at lower costs than they could individually. This collective purchasing power not only reduced the financial burden on farmers but also enable them to have better negotiation terms and enabling them to continue farming despite the economic downturn.

Example: The Farmers' Cooperative Association of Iowa (FCAI), established in the early 1920s, provided member farmers with access to discounted farm supplies. Through bulk purchasing, FCAI negotiated lower prices for its members, allowing farmers to stretch their limited budgets further during the Depression.

2. Marketing Products: Marketing cooperatives became instrumental in helping farmers secure fair prices for their produce amidst volatile market conditions. These cooperatives enabled farmers to aggregate their harvests and negotiate directly with buyers, bypassing traditional middlemen who often drove down

prices to their advantage.

Example: The California Fruit Growers Exchange, founded in 1893 (later renamed Sunkist Growers, Inc.), was a pioneering agricultural cooperative that marketed citrus fruits for its member growers. During the Great Depression, Sunkist facilitated collective marketing efforts, ensuring that its members received competitive prices and maintained market access despite economic turmoil. Sunkist Growers, Inc., began expanding its activities beyond collective marketing efforts in the early 1900s. Specifically, the cooperative started processing member farmers' fruit into juice and other products around 1908. This move allowed Sunkist to add value to the fruit and better manage supply. this adding value

contributed to its member farmers income increase, growth, success in the market and able to bring more income benefits to its member farmers.

3. Accessing Credit: Cooperative banks and credit unions provided essential financial services to farmers who were excluded from traditional banking institutions due to high-risk lending conditions. These cooperative financial institutions offered loans at lower interest rates, longer repayment terms, and more flexible collateral requirements tailored to the needs of agricultural producers.

Example:

The Farm Credit System (FCS), established in 1916, was a government-sponsored cooperative network of banks and lending associations designed to provide long-term credit to farmers. During the Great Depression, the FCS expanded its operations to meet the growing demand for agricultural loans, helping farmers refinance debt, purchase land, and invest in farm improvements (Farm Credit Administration, 2023).

National Cooperative Bank (NCB[7]): NCB is the only bank in the United States specifically dedicated to providing nationwide banking products and services to cooperatives and other member-owned organizations. Established by an act of Congress in 1978, NCB operates with the mission of supporting community development through cooperative principles. NCB is owned by its cooperative members. This ownership structure means that the bank operates for the benefit of these members rather than for outside investors.

Market Status:NCB has assets totaling approximately $8.4 billion, is a well-established financial institution with a strong presence in the cooperative sector. It is known for its specialized focus on cooperatives, housing associations, non-profits, and socially responsible businesses. NCB is a cooperative bank itself, meaning it operates for the benefit of its cooperative members rather than outside investors. NCB, provides specialized and member-focused services such as Commercial Banking Services, Specialized Cooperative Services, Advisory and Support Services (National Cooperative Bank, 2023).

Key Facts: NCB's mission is to support and expand the cooperative sector, promoting economic development and social impact. Member-Focused: Unlike traditional banks, NCB operates for the benefit of its members, who are also its customers. Nationwide Reach: NCB provides services across the United States, making it accessible to a wide range of cooperatives and member-owned organizations.

To make it concrete, for instance, during the Great Depression, farmers faced plummeting crop prices and mounting debt. Agricultural cooperatives provided crucial support in several key areas:

1. Lower-Cost Supplies: Cooperatives helped farmers purchase essential supplies like seeds, fertilizers, and equipment at reduced costs by buying in bulk and passing the savings onto their members.

2. Better Marketing Opportunities: By banding together, farmers could collectively market their products, securing better prices and more stable markets than they could individually.

3. Access to Credit: Cooperatives offered financial assistance by extending credit to farmers, which was especially critical when traditional banks were reluctant to lend.

4. Shared Resources, Knowledge and Machinery: Cooperatives facilitated the sharing of resources, such as machinery, storage, marketing and processing facilities and expertise, enabling farmers to improve their productivity, increase product shelf life and marketability, and adopt sustainability practices.

5. Risk Management: By pooling resources and working together, cooperatives provided a safety net that helped farmers manage the risks associated with post-harvest loss, volatile markets and environmental challenges.

Through these supports, agricultural cooperatives enabled farmers to unite and create a buffer against the worst impacts of the economic downturn, fostering resilience and promoting economic stability in rural communities.

In summary, during the early 20th century and particularly during the Great Depression, the access to finance system of Credit Unions in the United States demonstrated their pivotal role in assisting farmers. By facilitating collective action in purchasing supplies, marketing products, and accessing credit, these cooperatives provided farmers with the necessary tools to navigate economic hardships and sustain their livelihoods. This cooperative model not only bolstered individual farm resilience but also contributed to the broader stability and sustainability of rural economies across the country.

COOPERATIVES' ROLE BEYOND AGRICULTURAL ECONOMICS

The role of cooperatives in purchasing supplies, marketing products, and accessing credit was pivotal in the early 20th century, extending beyond agricultural activities to support urban producers and consumers as well. These three functions were interconnected and essential for the economic viability of both rural and urban populations.

1. Purchasing Supplies: Cooperatives facilitated the acquisition of essential supplies for urban producers and consumers by buying in bulk, thereby reducing costs. This collective purchasing power allowed members to obtain necessities like food, clothing, and household goods at lower prices, making essential items more affordable and accessible (Birchall, 2012).

2. Marketing Products: In urban areas, cooperatives helped producers market their goods more efficiently. By working together, members could reach broader markets, secure better prices, and ensure a consistent demand for their products. This collective marketing approach also helped build stronger, more recognizable brands, benefiting both producers and consumers (Hoyt, 1951).

3. Accessing Credit and Insurance: Access to credit and insurance was crucial for the economic stability of urban populations. Cooperatives provide financial services, including loans and insurance, to their members, who might otherwise struggle to obtain these services from traditional financial institutions. This support enabled urban producers to invest in their businesses, manage risks, and maintain financial stability (Gordon Nembhard, 2014).

Through these roles, cooperatives created a robust support system that not only aided individual members but also enhanced the overall economic health of urban communities. By fostering cooperation and collective action, cooperatives ensured that urban populations had access to necessary resources, stable markets, and financial security. In the early 20th century, cooperatives extended beyond agricultural activities to support urban producers and consumers as well. Good examples are:

Urban Example: Consumer Cooperatives

Park Slope Food Coop (Brooklyn, New York): Founded in 1973, the Park Slope Food Coop is one of the oldest and largest consumer cooperatives in the United States. It allows members to buy groceries and household goods at reduced prices by purchasing in bulk and eliminating middlemen. Members work a few hours each month, which helps keep costs low. This cooperative makes essential goods more affordable for working-class families in the community (Adams, 2013).

Figure 4: Facilities of Park Slope Food Coop

Source: https://www.foodcoop.com/

Urban Example: Craft Cooperatives

Greenbelt Cooperative (Greenbelt, Maryland): Founded in the 1930s as part of the Greenbelt community project, the Greenbelt Cooperative provided local artisans and small-scale producers with a platform to collectively market their crafts. This cooperative model increased the visibility and sales of local crafts, helping artisans reach a broader customer base and compete with larger retailers. Today, the Greenbelt Cooperative continues to support local producers and maintain the community's cooperative spirit (Kawano, 2013).

Figure 5: Facilities of Greenbelt housing Cooperative

Source: https://ghi.coop see GHI Promotional Video

Urban Example: Credit Unions
St. Mary's Bank Credit Union (Manchester, New Hampshire):

Founded in 1908, St. Mary's Bank Credit Union is the first credit union in the United States. It provided working-class immigrants and urban residents with access to affordable loans, savings accounts, and other financial services. By offering financial products that were often unavailable from traditional banks, St. Mary's Bank helped members achieve financial stability and economic mobility (NCUA, 2023).

Figure 6: Facilities of St. Mary's Bank

Source: https://www.stmarysbank.com/

These examples illustrate the diverse roles that urban cooperatives play in supporting their communities, from making everyday goods more affordable to providing platforms for local artisans and ensuring access to essential financial services.

Example of Retail Cooperative:

ACE Hardware is a retailer-owned cooperative founded in 1924 by Richard Hesse, E. Gunnard Lindquist, Frank Burke, and Oscar Fisher. It is owned by independent store owners and targets homeowners. ACE Hardware is a retailer-owned cooperative founded in 1924 by Richard Hesse, E. Gunnard Lindquist, Frank Burke, and Oscar Fisher. It is owned by independent store owners and targets homeowners, DIY enthusiasts, and small contractors. Today, it is a major player in the U.S. hardware retail market, one of the largest and most recognized hardware retailers Cooperative in the United States. known for its extensive network of over 5,000 stores and robust support system for its members (ACE Hardware, 2023).

Figure 7: Facilities of ACE Hardware

Source: https://www.acehardware.com/

The above facts demonstrated the Cooperative's versatility and resilience by extending their benefits beyond the agricultural sector to support urban producers, workers, and consumers. Through their strategic functions of purchasing supplies, marketing products, and accessing credit, cooperatives have provided vital economic support and stability to urban communities. These organizations have empowered individuals to collectively leverage their purchasing power, enhance market reach, and secure necessary financial services that might otherwise be inaccessible.

By fostering cooperation and mutual support, urban cooperatives have facilitated not only economic viability but also social cohesion and community resilience. They have proven essential in making everyday goods more affordable, promoting local artisans and small-scale producers, and offering financial services tailored to the needs of their members. The enduring success of examples like the Park Slope Food Coop, Greenbelt Cooperative, and St. Mary's Bank Credit Union underscores the transformative impact of cooperatives in urban settings.

In summary, cooperatives have played a crucial role in bolstering urban economies by ensuring access to essential resources, stabilizing markets, and providing financial security. Their continued relevance and adaptability highlight the importance of cooperative principles in fostering sustainable and inclusive economic development across diverse communities and economic sectors.

IV. Great Depression (1930s)

SURGE IN COOPERATIVE ACTIVITIES DURING THE GREAT DEPRESSION.

The Great Depression of the 1930s was a period of severe economic downturn, marked by widespread unemployment, bank failures, and a dramatic decline in industrial output. In response to these challenging conditions, cooperative activities surged as communities sought ways to support each other and mitigate the impacts of the economic crisis. Cooperatives emerged as practical solutions for individuals and families striving to maintain their livelihoods and access essential goods and services.

The economic hardships of the Great Depression underscored the vulnerabilities of relying solely on market-driven solutions and highlighted the benefits of cooperative models. People turned to cooperatives for mutual support, pooling resources to meet their needs and ensuring a more equitable distribution of goods and services.

ESTABLISHMENT OF CREDIT UNIONS, CONSUMER COOPERATIVES, AND RURAL ELECTRIC COOPERATIVES

Several types of cooperatives saw significant growth during the Great Depression:

1. Credit Unions: As traditional banks failed and credit became scarce, credit unions gained prominence. These member-owned financial cooperatives provided a critical source of affordable credit to individuals and small businesses. ng>Impact, Credit unions offered loans at lower interest rates than commercial banks and were more willing to lend to people with limited collateral. Legislation and the establishment of the Federal Credit Union Act in 1934 further facilitated the growth of credit unions by providing a federal charter and regulatory framework (Federal Credit Union

Act, 1934).

2. Consumer Cooperatives: Consumer cooperatives allow individuals to pool their purchasing power to buy goods in bulk at reduced prices. These cooperatives operate grocery stores, supply depots, and other retail establishments that provide essential goods to members at lower costs than commercial outlets. By eliminating the profit motive and focusing on member needs, consumer cooperatives help families stretch their limited resources during the economic crisis (Birchall, 2012).

3. Rural Electric Cooperatives: Many rural areas in the United States lacked access to electricity during the early 20th century. The establishment of rural electric cooperatives was a response to this issue. These cooperatives were formed to bring electricity to rural communities that private utility companies deemed unprofitable to serve. The Rural Electrification Act of 1936 provided federal loans to support the development of these cooperatives, enabling widespread electrification of rural America. Access to electricity revolutionized rural life, improving productivity, health, and quality of life (Rural Electrification Act, 1936).

These cooperative initiatives were vital in helping communities weather the economic storm of the Great Depression, demonstrating the resilience and adaptability of cooperative models in times of crisis.

NEW DEAL POLICIES AND GOVERNMENT SUPPORT FOR COOPERATIVES

The New Deal, implemented by President Franklin D. Roosevelt's administration, included several policies and programs that supported the growth of cooperatives. Recognizing the potential of cooperatives to aid in economic recovery and improve living standards, the federal government provided significant assistance to these enterprises.

1. Federal Credit Union Act (1934): This act established a system of federally chartered credit unions, providing a legal framework and regulatory oversight. It facilitated the creation and expansion of credit unions across the country, ensuring that affordable credit was available to more Americans while also guaranteeing depositors' savings (Federal Credit Union Act, 1934).

2. Rural Electrification Act (1936): This legislation aimed to bring electricity to rural areas through the establishment of rural electric cooperatives. The act provided low-interest loans to cooperatives, enabling the construction of electrical infrastructure in underserved regions. The widespread electrification that followed transformed rural economies and improved the quality of life for millions of Americans (Rural Electrification Act, 1936).

3. New Deal Agencies: Various New Deal agencies, such as the Farm Security Administration (FSA) and the Works Progress Administration (WPA), supported cooperative initiatives. These agencies provided technical assistance, funding, and resources to cooperatives, helping them establish and expand their operations (Adams, 2013).

CONTRIBUTION OF COOPERATIVES TO ECONOMIC RECOVERY

Cooperatives made substantial contributions to the economic recovery during the Great Depression. By providing affordable credit, essential goods, and access to electricity, cooperatives helped stabilize communities and support local economies. They enabled individuals and families to maintain their livelihoods, reduced the financial burden on households, and fostered a sense of collective responsibility and mutual aid.

- Credit Unions offered a lifeline to individuals and small businesses, ensuring that they could access the credit needed to sustain their operations and meet their financial obligations (Gordon Nembhard, 2014).

• Consumer Cooperatives helped families secure basic necessities at lower costs, stretching their limited resources and mitigating the impacts of unemployment and wage cuts (Kawano, 2013).

• Rural Electric Cooperatives played a transformative role in rural communities by bringing electricity to areas previously without access. Electrification boosted agricultural productivity, supported new industries, and improved living conditions. It also facilitated the development of infrastructure and services, such as schools and healthcare facilities, contributing to long-term economic and social development (Paris, 2019).

In summary, the Great Depression was a pivotal period for the cooperative movement in the United States. Cooperatives surged in response to economic hardship, with credit unions, consumer cooperatives, and rural electric cooperatives playing critical roles in supporting communities. The New Deal policies and government support for cooperatives further enhanced their capacity to contribute to economic recovery, demonstrating the resilience and effectiveness of the cooperative model during times of crisis.

Practical example to justify the cooperative enterprise role and activities during the Great Depression and the establishment of credit unions, consumer cooperatives, and rural electric cooperatives:

Example: Rural Electric Cooperatives

During the Great Depression, many rural areas in the United States lacked access to electricity, which was critical for economic development and quality of life improvements. Private utility companies often deemed rural electrification unprofitable, leaving millions of Americans in the dark. In response to this critical need, rural electric cooperatives emerged as a transformative solution:

1. Formation and Purpose: Rural electric cooperatives (RECs) were formed by rural residents who banded together to bring electricity to their communities. These cooperatives were typically organized as non-profit entities owned and governed by their members residents and farmers who lacked access to investor-owned utilities.

Example: The Central Electric Power Cooperative in Missouri (CEPC) was established in 1938 to serve rural communities across the state. Initially formed by local farmers and residents who pooled resources, CEPC received support through the Rural Electrification Administration (REA), a New Deal agency created in 1935. REA provided low-interest loans and technical assistance to help cooperatives build electrical infrastructure and bring power to rural areas (Cronon, 1991).

Figure 8: Facilities of CEPC

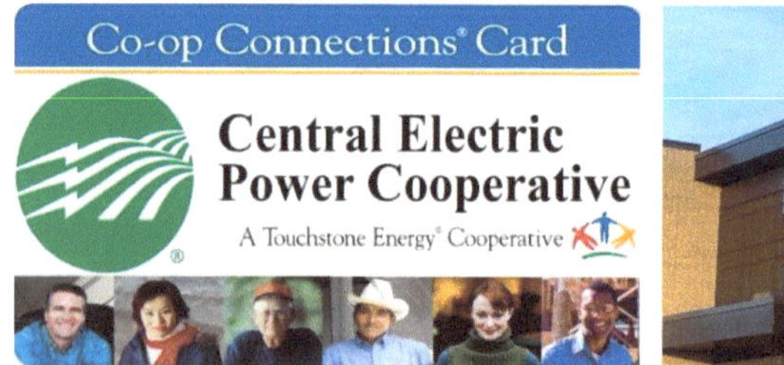

Source: https://www.cepc.net

2. Impact on Economic Development: Rural electrification had profound economic implications. It enabled farmers to modernize agricultural practices, improving productivity and reducing labor-intensive methods. Access to electricity also facilitated the adoption of new technologies, such as electric pumps for irrigation, refrigeration for food preservation, and electric motors for farm machinery.

Example: In the Midwest, cooperatives like CEPC facilitated the installation of electrical grids that powered irrigation systems, dairy operations, and grain processing facilities. This infrastructure not only boosted agricultural output but also supported the growth of local economies by attracting new industries and businesses.

3. Community Resilience and Social Benefits: Beyond economic gains, rural electric cooperatives fostered community resilience and social cohesion. Member-owners actively participated in the governance of their cooperatives, ensuring that decisions were made in the best interest of the community rather than profit motives alone. Cooperatives provided more than just electricity; they became centers for community gatherings, education on electrical safety, and forums for discussing local issues.

Example: CEPC organized educational workshops for farmers on the efficient use of electricity in agriculture, demonstrating techniques for maximizing energy efficiency and minimizing costs. These initiatives not only empowered farmers with knowledge but also strengthened the cooperative spirit within rural communities.

4. Government Support and Policy Impact: The establishment of rural electric cooperatives was greatly facilitated by New Deal policies aimed at rural development. The Rural Electrification Act (REA) of 1936 provided critical financial, technical assistance and regulatory support to cooperatives, enabling them to undertake large-scale electrification projects that private utilities had neglected.

Example: Through REA funding, cooperatives like CEPC expanded their service territories, bringing electricity to remote areas previously deemed unprofitable by private companies. This federal support transformed the lives of millions of rural Americans, bridging the "electricity divide" and laying the groundwork for long-term economic prosperity.

In summary, rural electric cooperatives exemplify the surge in cooperative activities during the Great Depression and illustrate the profound impact of cooperative models on economic development and community resilience. By empowering rural residents to take control of their energy future, these cooperatives not only brought light to darkened homes but also illuminated pathways to prosperity and social progress in rural America. The success of rural electric cooperatives underscored the effectiveness of cooperative principles in addressing critical infrastructure needs and fostering sustainable community development during times of national crisis.

V. Post-World War II Era

CONTINUED IMPORTANCE OF THE COOPERATIVE
MODEL AFTER WWII

In the aftermath of World War II, the cooperative model continued to play a vital role in the United States. The period following the war was marked by significant economic growth and development, and cooperatives were essential in supporting this progress, particularly in rural areas. The cooperative model's emphasis on democratic governance, member ownership, and community focus made it well-suited to address the economic and social challenges of the post-war era.

The federal government and various states continued to support cooperatives, recognizing their potential to contribute to economic stability and growth. Cooperatives provided essential services and opportunities for economic participation of millions of Americans, fostering a sense of empowerment and community solidarity.

Example: Rural Electric Cooperatives

A prime example of the continued importance of cooperatives after WWII is the success and expansion of rural electric cooperatives. These cooperatives, initially established during the New Deal, played a crucial role in electrifying rural America. Before their establishment, many rural areas lacked access to electricity, which hindered economic development and quality of life.

After WWII, the federal government and various states continued to support these cooperatives, recognizing their potential to contribute to economic stability and growth. With the help of federal loans and technical assistance, rural electric cooperatives expanded their reach, bringing electricity to remote and underserved areas.

MODERNIZATION OF AGRICULTURE THROUGH COOPERATIVES

One of the most significant impacts of cooperatives in the post-war era was the modernization of agriculture. Agricultural cooperatives played a crucial role in helping farmers adapt to new technologies and practices, which were essential for increasing productivity and efficiency. These cooperatives provided farmers with access to modern equipment, advanced farming techniques, and better-quality inputs such as seeds and fertilizers.

Cooperatives also facilitated the adoption of scientific farming methods, which contributed to higher crop yields and improved livestock production. By pooling resources and sharing knowledge, farmers were able to benefit from economies of scale and reduce the risks associated with farming. Agricultural cooperatives also helped farmers navigate the complexities of market fluctuations, ensuring that they received fair prices for their products.

Example: Land O'Lakes Cooperative

A notable example is the Land O'Lakes cooperative, which was instrumental in modernizing dairy farming practices in the United States. Founded in 1921, Land O'Lakes expanded significantly after World War II, providing its members with access to cutting-edge agricultural technologies and resources.

- Access to Modern Equipment and Techniques,Land O'Lakes facilitated the adoption of modern equipment such as milking machines and refrigerated storage, which were essential for increasing milk production and ensuring the quality of dairy products. By pooling resources, cooperative members could afford equipment that would have been prohibitively expensive for individual farmers.

- Scientific Farming Methods and Education,the cooperative also played a critical role in educating farmers about advanced farming techniques. Through workshops, training sessions, and informational publications, Land O'Lakes disseminated knowledge about scientific farming methods, including improved breeding practices, disease control, and effective feed management. This education led to higher dairy cows' health improvement, animal feed crop yields and improved livestock production.
- Economies of Scale and Risk Reduction,by working together, farmers in the cooperative benefited from economies of scale. They could purchase inputs such as seeds and fertilizers in bulk at lower prices, reducing their overall costs. Additionally, the cooperative provided a platform for sharing knowledge and best practices, which helped mitigate the risks associated with farming.
- Market Stability and Fair Prices,Agricultural cooperatives like Land O'Lakes also helped farmers navigate market fluctuations. By collectively processing & marketing their products, cooperatives proved that farmers able and could negotiate better prices and ensure a stable income for their members. This collective bargaining power was particularly important during times of economic uncertainty, providing a buffer against volatile market conditions.

Land O'Lakes is a prime example of how cooperatives can stabilize markets and secure fair prices for farmers. Land O'Lakes is a member-owned cooperative that processes and markets dairy products. Here are some specific ways Land O'Lakes has supported its members:

- Processing Facilities: Land O'Lakes operates multiple processing plants, where members' milk is turned into high-quality butter, cheese, and other dairy products. This not only adds value to the raw milk but also ensures consistent product quality and branding.

- Marketing Strategies: The cooperative employs sophisticated marketing strategies to promote its products nationally and internationally. By leveraging its strong brand reputation, Land O'Lakes secures premium prices for its products.
- Price Negotiation: With its significant market presence, Land O'Lakes can negotiate better terms with retailers and distributors, ensuring that its members receive fair compensation for their produce.
- Market Intelligence: The cooperative provides members with insights into market trends and pricing, helping them make informed production decisions and plans.

Figure 9: Products of Land O'Lakes

Source: https://www.landolakesinc.com/

Agricultural cooperatives were pivotal in modernizing farming practices in the post-war era. By providing access to modern equipment, advanced techniques, and high-quality inputs, cooperatives like Land O'Lakes significantly increased agricultural productivity and efficiency. Through education and resource pooling, they helped farmers adopt scientific farming methods, benefit from economies of scale, and reduce risks. Moreover, these cooperatives ensured that farmers received fair prices for their products, contributing to the overall stability and growth of the agricultural sector.

In conclusion, the post-World War II era highlighted the continued importance of cooperatives in the United States. Through initiatives like rural electric cooperatives and agricultural cooperatives such as

Land O'Lakes, cooperatives played a crucial role in modernizing agriculture, stabilizing local economies, and improving the quality of life for millions of Americans. By fostering community solidarity and economic participation, cooperatives proved to be resilient and effective models for addressing the challenges of the post-war era.

EXPANSION OF ACCESS TO ELECTRICITY AND IMPROVEMENT IN LIVING STANDARDS

The expansion of access to electricity was another significant achievement of cooperatives in the post-war era. Rural electric cooperatives, established during the New Deal, continued to play a critical role in bringing electricity to underserved rural areas. By the 1950s, these cooperatives had succeeded in electrifying most of rural America, transforming the lives of millions of people.

Access to electricity had profound effects on rural communities, improving living standards and enabling economic development. Electrification allowed for the modernization of homes, schools, and healthcare facilities, enhancing the quality of life. It also supported the growth of rural industries and businesses, creating new employment opportunities and stimulating local economies.

Example: NRECA and Rural Electrification

The National Rural Electric Cooperative Association (NRECA), founded in 1942, provides an excellent example of how cooperatives expanded access to electricity. NRECA coordinated the efforts of hundreds of rural electric cooperatives, facilitating the sharing of resources, knowledge, and technical expertise.

Figure 10: Facilities of NRECA

Source: https://www.electric.coop

- **Transformation of Rural Communities**

Access to electricity had profound effects on rural communities, improving living standards and enabling economic development. Electrification allowed for the modernization of homes, schools, and healthcare facilities, significantly enhancing the quality of life for rural residents. Homes were equipped with electric lights, appliances, and heating systems, making daily life more convenient and comfortable (National Rural Electric Cooperative Association, 2021).

- **Economic Development and Modernization**

Electrification also supported the growth of rural industries and businesses, creating new employment opportunities and stimulating local economies. For instance, farms could use electric pumps for irrigation, electric tools and machinery for production, and refrigeration for preserving produce and dairy products. These advancements led to increased agricultural productivity and efficiency, which were crucial for the economic sustainability of rural areas (U.S. Department of Agriculture, 2014).

- **Improvement in Public Services**

Public services in rural areas also saw significant improvements due to electrification. Schools were able to use electric lighting and equipment, enabling better educational environments and extended study hours. Healthcare facilities could operate modern medical equipment, store medicines properly with refrigeration, and provide more comprehensive care to patients. These enhancements in public services contributed to better health outcomes and educational achievements in rural communities (U.S. Department of Agriculture, 2014).

In summary, the expansion of access to electricity through rural electric cooperatives was a monumental achievement in the post-war era. Organizations like the NRECA played a pivotal role in this transformation, ensuring that even the most remote areas of the United States benefited from electrification. The impact on rural communities was profound, with significant improvements in living standards, economic development, and public services. Electrification modernized homes, schools, and healthcare facilities created new employment opportunities, and stimulated local economies, thereby transforming the lives of millions and contributing to the overall growth and prosperity of rural America.

GROWTH OF HOUSING COOPERATIVES AND WORKER COOPERATIVES

The post-war era also saw the growth of housing cooperatives and worker cooperatives, which addressed housing shortages and provided alternative employment opportunities.

1. Housing Cooperatives:

- Context and Need: In the post-World War II era, the United States faced significant housing shortages as returning soldiers and their families sought affordable and stable housing. The conventional housing market struggled to meet this demand, leading to the emergence of cooperative housing as an alternative solution (Birchall, 2012).
  Example: The Mutual Housing Association of New York (MHANY): Established in 1952, MHANY addressed the housing needs of low-

income families in Brooklyn. Formed as a cooperative, MHANY allowed residents to collectively own and manage apartment buildings, providing affordable rental housing while promoting community stability and resident engagement. Members of MHANY had a say in how their buildings were managed and benefited from stable rents and improved living conditions compared to conventional rental housing (Shaffer, 2006).

Figure 11: Facilities of MHANY

Source: https://www.mutualhousingny.org

● Ownership and Management: Housing cooperatives operated on the principle of democratic control, where residents (often referred to as members) jointly owned the cooperative and made decisions through a democratic governance structure. This ownership model ensured that housing decisions were made in the best interest of the residents rather than profit-driven motives (Shaffer, 2006).

Example: Cooperative members of MHANY: They participated in regular meetings where they discussed maintenance issues, budgeting, and community programs. This participatory approach empowered residents and fostered a sense of community pride and responsibility, leading to well-maintained properties and improved living standards (Shaffer, 2006).

• Affordability and Stability: Housing cooperatives provided a stable and affordable housing option for members. By pooling financial resources and collectively owning the property, cooperative members could keep housing costs lower than market rates, making housing more accessible to low-income and middle-income families (Birchall, 2012).

Example: MHANY: Beyond economic benefits, housing cooperatives like MHANY contributed to community development and social cohesion. Residents had opportunities to participate in social activities, educational programs, and community events organized by the cooperative. This sense of belonging fostered strong neighborhood bonds and improved the overall quality of life for cooperative members (Birchall, 2012).

• Community Benefits: Today, manages over 1,500 affordable housing units, providing stable and affordable homes to low- and moderate-income families. Continues to develop new housing projects to meet the ongoing demand for affordable housing in New York City. Beyond economic benefits, housing cooperatives like MHANY contributed to community development and social cohesion. Residents had opportunities to participate in social activities, educational programs, and community events organized by the cooperative. This sense of belonging fostered strong neighborhood bonds and improved the overall quality of life for cooperative members. Organized neighborhood cleanup days, youth programs, and adult education classes in collaboration with local organizations. These initiatives not only enriched the lives of residents but also strengthened community resilience and engagement, creating a supportive environment for families to thrive (Shaffer, 2006).

2. Worker Cooperatives:

• Context and Need: Worker cooperatives gained traction as a means of providing stable and equitable employment opportunities. In a worker cooperative, employees collectively own and manage the business, sharing in both decision-making and profits. This model empowered workers, promoted job satisfaction, and reduced income inequality (Greenberg, 1986).

Example: Cooperative Home Care Associates (CHCA): Founded in 1985 in the South Bronx, New York, CHCA became one of the largest worker cooperatives in the United States. It was established to provide home care services while creating quality jobs for low-income women, predominantly women of color. The cooperative model allowed these workers to have a say in their working conditions and share in the profits of the business (Gordon, 2014).

Figure 12: Facilities of CHCA

Source: https://www.chcany.org

• Ownership and Management: In worker cooperatives, employees are also owners, participating in decision-making processes and in processes and sharing in the profits and risks of the business. This ownership model fosters a sense of responsibility and motivation among workers (Greenberg, 1986).

Example: CHCA: The workers at CHCA participated in governance through a democratic voting system. This model not only ensured fair treatment and better working conditions but also increased job satisfaction and retention rates (Gordon, 2014).

● Economic and Social Impact: Worker cooperatives like CHCA contributed to economic diversification and resilience. They provided equitable employment opportunities and promoted community development through fair wages and benefits (Greenberg, 1986).

Example: CHCA: Offered its worker-owners extensive training and career advancement opportunities, leading to professional growth and improved quality of care for clients and service satisfaction. The cooperative's success demonstrated the potential of worker cooperatives to create sustainable and fair employment in various sectors (Gordon, 2014).

Today, Cooperative Home Care Associates (CHCA) is one of the largest worker cooperatives in the United States, remains a shining example of the Worker cooperative model's potential to provide equitable employment and high-quality services, created employment for 2,000 worker-owners. By empowering its worker-owners through democratic governance and profit-sharing, CHCA fosters a supportive and motivated workforce dedicated to delivering exceptional home care through providing extensive continues training programs to ensure high-quality care and professional development for its employees. Training includes personal care, advanced clinical skills, and leadership development. Its ongoing commitment to community development, advocacy, and innovation positions CHCA as a crucial player in the home care industry and a beacon for cooperative enterprises nationwide(Gordon, 2014).

Summary, the post-World War II era was a period of significant growth and development for cooperatives in the United States. Housing cooperatives provided affordable, stable housing solutions, and worker cooperatives offered equitable employment opportunities. Throughout this period, the cooperative model demonstrated its capacity to address economic and social challenges, fostering community development and economic self-reliance. Examples like MHANY and CHCA illustrate how cooperatives continued to play a vital role in improving living standards and providing stable employment, thereby contributing to the overall growth and prosperity of American society.

VI. Today's U.S. Economy

COOPERATIVE ENTERPRISES IN THE US MODERN ECONOMY

In today's U.S. economy, cooperative enterprises continue to play a crucial role across various sectors. These member-owned businesses remain significant due to their ability to address contemporary economic challenges, promote sustainable development, and foster economic resilience. Cooperatives have adapted to the modern economic landscape while maintaining their core principles of democratic governance, member ownership, and community focus. They provide essential services, create economic opportunities, and contribute to the well-being of their members and communities.

MODERNIZING AGRICULTURE AND IMPROVING LIVING STANDARDS

Modernizing Agriculture: Agricultural cooperatives are pivotal in modernizing farming practices and ensuring the sustainability of rural economies. They provide farmers with access to cutting-edge technology, high-quality inputs, and advanced farming techniques. By pooling resources and knowledge, cooperatives help farmers increase productivity, reduce costs, and improve the quality of their products. This collective approach enables small and medium-sized farmers to compete in larger markets, ensuring their economic viability.

Example: Ocean Spray Cranberries, Inc.

Owned by over 700 cranberry growers in various states and more than 50 Florida grapefruit growers[8], Ocean Spray helps farmers access markets and resources to remain competitive. Ocean Spray is North America's leading producer of canned and bottled juices, with peak revenue of $2.0 billion in 2023 and 2,000 employees. The company holds a 60% market share of the U.S. cranberry juice market and a 70% share of the fresh cranberry market. Today, Ocean Spray is considered one of the most innovative and entrepreneurial companies in the U.S.

Figure 13: Products of Ocean Spray

Source: https://www.oceanspray.com

1. Expanding Electricity Access: Rural electric cooperatives continue to play a vital role in providing reliable and affordable electricity to rural communities. They invest in infrastructure upgrades and renewable energy projects, ensuring that rural areas have access to modern and sustainable energy solutions. These cooperatives are at the forefront of initiatives to expand broadband internet access in rural areas, bridging the digital divide and promoting economic development.

Example: Mid-Carolina Electric Cooperative (MCEC), Founded: 1939, located in South Carolina, USA. MCEC has been instrumental in expanding electricity access to rural areas in South Carolina since its founding. Initially established to provide electricity to farms and rural households that were not being served by investor-owned utilities, MCEC continues to invest in electricity.

Renewable Energy Projects: MCEC has undertaken several renewable energy projects, including the development of solar farms and the integration of wind energy. These projects not only provide clean energy to its members but also contribute to the cooperative's goal of sustainability. For instance, MCEC has partnered with other cooperatives in the state to develop large-scale solar projects, making renewable energy more accessible and affordable for rural communities.

Figure 14: Facility of MCEC

Mid-Carolina
ELECTRIC COOPERATIVE

Source : https://www.mcecoop.com

2. Broadband Internet Access: Recognizing the importance of internet access for economic development, MCEC has also been a leader in expanding broadband services in rural areas. In partnership with local and state agencies, MCEC has launched initiatives to bring high-speed internet to underserved regions, helping to bridge the digital divide. This access to broadband internet has facilitated telemedicine, remote learning, and other essential services, thereby promoting economic and social development in these communities.

3. Economic Development: By providing reliable electricity and internet services, MCEC has played a significant role in fostering economic development in rural South Carolina. Businesses, schools, and healthcare facilities have been able to thrive thanks to the infrastructure and services provided by the cooperative. MCEC's efforts have helped to attract new businesses to the area, creating jobs and boosting the local economy.

4. Community Engagement: MCEC also engages with its members through educational programs and community events, promoting energy efficiency and sustainability. The cooperative's commitment to its members is evident in its responsive customer service and continuous efforts to improve the quality of life in the communities it serves.

• Summary: Mid-Carolina Electric Cooperative today manages total assets of approximately $350 million, these assets include the cooperative's electrical infrastructure, such as transmission and distribution lines, substations, and renewable energy installations. MCEC is serving over 50,000 members and 58,000+ accounts serviced. exemplifies the ongoing importance of rural electric cooperatives in expanding electricity access and promoting economic development in rural areas. Through investments in infrastructure upgrades, renewable energy projects, and broadband internet access, MCEC ensures that rural communities have access to modern and sustainable energy solutions. The cooperative's efforts contribute to the overall well-being and prosperity of its members, demonstrating the vital role that rural electric cooperatives continue to play in the United States.

5. Improving Living Standards: Cooperatives contribute to improving living standards in rural areas by providing essential services such as healthcare, education, and housing. Housing cooperatives offer affordable and quality housing options, ensuring that rural residents have access to stable and secure living conditions. Additionally, cooperatives often support community development projects, such as building community centers and recreational facilities, enhancing the overall quality of life in rural areas.

Examples of cooperatives in the U.S. that **Provide Essential Urban Services** like **Healthcare and Education**:

Healthcare Cooperatives

1. HealthPartners:

Services: HealthPartners is located in Twin Cities, Minnesota, a large consumer-governed nonprofit health care organization offering comprehensive health services, including medical, dental, and insurance coverage. They operate several clinics and hospitals in urban areas, focusing on integrated care and preventive health.

Figure 15: Facilities of HealthPartners

Source : https://www.healthpartners.com

2. Harlem United:

Services: Harlem United is located in New York City, New York, a community-based health cooperative that provides a range of health services, including primary care, dental care, behavioral health services, and supportive housing. They focus on serving underserved urban populations, particularly those affected by HIV/AIDS.

Figure 16: Facilities of Harlem United

Source: https://www.harlemunited.org

3. Common Ground Health Cooperative:

This cooperative is located in Milwaukee, Wisconsin, it offers health insurance plans to individuals and small businesses, ensuring access to affordable healthcare in urban areas. They partner with local healthcare providers to deliver high-quality care.

Figure 17: Facilities of Harlem United

Source: https://commongroundhealthcare.org

Education Cooperatives
4. Urban School Food Alliance:

This cooperative locates in Various urban districts across the U.S, it brings together large urban school districts to improve the quality and affordability of school meals. By pooling their purchasing power, they can negotiate better prices and higher standards for food served to students in urban schools.

Figure 18: Facilities of Urban School Food Alliance

Source: https://urbanschoolfoodalliance.org

5. The Cooperative Education Services Agency (CESA):

While CESAs serve both rural and urban areas, they play a crucial role in urban education by providing shared services such as special education, professional development, and technology integration. They help urban schools access resources and support that enhance educational outcomes. It is located in Various locations of Wisconsin.

Figure 19: Facilities of CESA

Source : https://dpi.wi.gov/wise/data-elements/CESA

6. Cooperative Educational Services (CES):

CES located in Trumbull, Connecticut & it provides a range of educational services to urban school districts, including special education programs, professional development for educators, and technology integration. Their goal is to enhance educational opportunities and outcomes in urban schools by leveraging cooperative efforts.

Figure 20: Facilities of CES

Source: https://www.ces.org

These cooperatives demonstrate how collective action can enhance access to essential services in urban areas, improving the overall quality of life for residents.

Some specific examples of cooperatives that Provide Essential Rural Services like Healthcare and Education in the U.S.:

Healthcare Cooperatives

1. Group Health Cooperative of South-Central Wisconsin (GHC-SCW):

GHC-SCW is in Madison, Wisconsin and is a member-owned, nonprofit health cooperative providing comprehensive health services, including primary care, specialty care, and behavioral health services. They focus on preventive care and have multiple clinics serving the rural communities of South-Central Wisconsin.

Figure 21: Facilities of GHC-SCW

Source: https://ghcscw.com/

2. Mountain Health Cooperative:

This cooperative is located in Idaho and Montana, it offers health insurance plans to individuals and families, ensuring access to affordable healthcare in rural areas. They work with local providers to deliver quality care and emphasize preventive health measures.

Figure 22: Facilities of Mountain Health Cooperative

Source: https://mountainhealth.coop

3. Community Health Partners Cooperative (CHP):

CHP operates health centers in rural areas of Montana, offering medical, dental, and behavioral health services on a sliding fee scale. Their goal is to provide comprehensive care regardless of the patient's ability to pay, ensuring rural residents have access to necessary health services.

Figure 23: Facilities of CHP

Source: https://www.chpwa.org

Education Cooperatives

1. Central Minnesota Educational Research and Development Council (CMERDC):

CMERDC is located in St. Cloud, Minnesota, it is a cooperative that provides a variety of educational services to rural school districts, including professional development, technology support, and curriculum resources. They help schools improve educational outcomes by sharing resources and expertise.

Figure 24: Facilities of CMERDC

Source: https://cmerdc.org

2. Southwest Educational Development Center (SEDC):

SEDC is located in Cedar City, Utah, it is a cooperative that supports rural school districts in Southwestern Utah. They offer services such as instructional technology support, professional development for teachers, and special education services. SEDC helps small, rural schools access resources that would be challenging to obtain individually.

Figure 25: Facilities of SERDC

Source: https://sedck12.org

3. Missouri Research and Education Network (MOREnet):

MOREnet is located in Missouri, it is a cooperative network that provides internet access, technical support, and training to schools, libraries, and other educational institutions in rural Missouri. By pooling resources, they ensure rural communities have the connectivity and technology needed for modern education.

Figure 26: Facilities of MOREnet

Source: https://www.more.net

These cooperatives illustrate the power of collective action in improving access to essential services in rural areas, contributing to healthier and more educated communities.

Summary, Cooperatives play a crucial role in providing essential services such as healthcare and education across both urban and rural areas in the United States. By leveraging collective action and member ownership, these cooperatives ensure that communities have access to necessary services that might otherwise be unavailable or unaffordable. These cooperatives demonstrate the power of collective effort in addressing critical needs in both urban and rural communities. By providing essential services such as healthcare and education, they contribute to improved living standards, enhanced community development, and greater access to necessary resources. In rural areas, they often serve as the primary providers of these services, filling gaps that might otherwise leave residents underserved. In urban areas, they enhance the quality and affordability of services, addressing the unique challenges faced by densely populated regions.

ENHANCEMENT OF ACCESS TO FINANCE

1. Credit Unions: Credit unions are a cornerstone of the cooperative financial sector, providing affordable and accessible financial services to millions of Americans. These member-owned institutions offer a wide range of services, including savings accounts, loans, mortgages, and financial education. Credit unions prioritize the financial well-being of their members, offering lower fees and better interest rates than traditional banks. They play a crucial role in promoting financial inclusion, especially for underserved populations, by providing access to credit and helping members build financial security. To mention some examples of US Credit Unions

Navy Federal Credit Union: The largest credit union in the U.S., Navy Federal serves over 13.2 million members, primarily military personnel and their families, operating nationwide. It offers a comprehensive range of financial services, including savings and checking accounts, loans, mortgages, credit cards, and financial education. Navy Federal prioritizes low fees and competitive interest rates, promoting financial well-being among its members. It has created Approximately $170.8 billion in assets, with 355 branches and 22 of them are Overseas with 30,000ATM and employs 24,300 people.

Figure 27: Facilities of Navy Federal Credit Union

Source: https://www.navyfederal.org

Alliant Credit Union: is one of the largest credit unions in the country, operate in Chicago, Illinois (and nationwide), providing services to over 600,000 members. It offers savings and checking accounts, personal loans, mortgages, and investment services. Alliant focuses on delivering high-interest savings accounts and low-interest loans, helping members achieve financial security. It has created approximately $18 billion in assets and employs more than 500 people.

Figure 28: Facilities of Alliant Credit Union

Source: https://www.alliantcreditunion.org

Self-Help Credit Union: specializes in serving 150,000 low-income members and underserved communities, operates in Durham, North Carolina (and other states). It offers a variety of financial products, including savings accounts, personal and home loans, and small business loans. Self-help focuses on economic development and financial inclusion, providing access to credit and financial education to those who might be excluded from traditional banking services. It has created approximately $2 billion in assets and employs more than 300 people.

Figure 29: Facilities of Self-Help Credit Union

Source : https://www.self-helpfcu.org

2. Insurance Cooperatives: have their roots in the broader cooperative movement that gained momentum in the 19th century. The first modern insurance cooperatives began emerging in the late 1800s and early 1900s, inspired by the success of other cooperative enterprises. Insurance Cooperatives are owned by their policyholders rather than shareholders. Today, insurance cooperatives continue to provide essential services to their members, focusing on affordability, accessibility, and member-driven governance. They remain an important part of the cooperative sector, contributing to the financial well-being and security of their members while supporting community development.

Coop Insurance Companies was established in 1915, founded in Middlebury, Vermont, to provide insurance solutions tailored to the needs of rural and agricultural communities. Today, continues to offer auto, home, farm, and business insurance. The cooperative remains focused on customer service and community support, serving members primarily in Vermont and New Hampshire. There are many insurance cooperatives in all states.

Figure 30: Facilities of Coop Insurance Companies

Source : https://www.co-opinsurance.com

Group Health Cooperative (GHC)

It was started in 1976, and established in Madison, Wisconsin, to provide high-quality healthcare coverage with an emphasis on preventive care and member health education. Today, GHC serves

thousands of members, offering a variety of health insurance plans including individual, family, and employer plans. It continues to focus on healthcare access and education for its members.

Figure 31: Facilities of Coop Insurance Companies

Source: https://ghcscw.com

National Rural Electric Cooperative Association (NRECA)

Started in 1942 to support rural electric cooperatives by providing comprehensive insurance benefits to their employees, Today NRECA offers health and retirement plans for employees of member electric cooperatives, supporting thousands of employees nationwide.

Figure 32: Facilities of NRECA

Source: https://www.electric.coop

Nationwide Mutual Insurance Company

Founded in 1926 as the Farm Bureau Mutual Automobile Insurance Company in Columbus, Ohio, to provide affordable auto insurance to farmers. Nationwide is owned by its policyholders, also known as members. Today, it is one of the largest insurance and financial services companies in the U.S. It offers a wide range of insurance products, including auto, home, life, and business insurance, as well as retirement and investment services. The company serves millions of policyholders across the country and remains a mutual company, prioritizing the needs of its members.

Figure 33: Facilities of Nationwide Insurance Company

Source : https://www.nationwide.com

Overall, insurance cooperatives like Co-op Insurance Companies, Group Health Cooperatives, and Nationwide Mutual Insurance Companies exemplify the cooperative principles of member ownership, democratic governance, and community focus. They provide essential insurance services that enhance financial well-being and security for their members as policy owners while also contributing to the development and support of their communities.

SIGNIFICANCE OF COOPERATIVE ENTERPRISES IN RURAL AND URBAN ECONOMICS

Cooperative enterprises are significant job creators, providing employment opportunities in both rural and urban areas in today's U.S. Their business model prioritizes sustainable growth and long-term stability, contributing to more than 2 million secured jobs and economic resilience in the U.S. alone.

1. Rural Employment and Cooperatives

In rural areas, cooperatives play a crucial role in enhancing local economies and providing employment opportunities. Agricultural cooperatives, rural electric cooperatives, and other community-focused cooperatives contribute significantly to the economic vitality of rural communities by achieving better market access, negotiating better prices, and sharing production costs. Additionally, they create jobs and improve skill levels for local job seekers through various initiatives.

- **Agricultural Cooperatives**

Agricultural cooperatives are formed by farmers who pool their resources for collective benefits. Their contributions in today's U.S. economy include:

- Market Access and Price Negotiation: By banding together, farmers are able to access larger markets and negotiate better prices for their products, ensuring a more stable income.

● Job Creation: These cooperatives generate employment within the farming sector and in related industries such as processing, transportation, and marketing.

● Skill Development: They offer training programs in modern agricultural techniques, financial management, and sustainable practices, enhancing the skills and job prospects of their members.

- **Rural Electric Cooperatives.**

Rural electric cooperatives are member-owned utilities that provide electricity to rural communities. Their impact includes:

● Infrastructure Development: By extending electrical infrastructure, these cooperatives create jobs in construction, maintenance, and administration.

● Economic Growth: Reliable electricity supports local businesses and attracts new enterprises, fostering economic growth and creating further employment opportunities.

● Technical Training: They offer training programs in electrical maintenance and other technical skills, improving residents' employment prospects.

- **Community-Focused Cooperatives**

Other community-focused cooperatives, such as credit unions, health cooperatives, and craft cooperatives, also play a vital role in rural areas.

● Job Creation: These cooperatives create jobs in diverse sectors, including finance, healthcare, and artisanal crafts, supporting varied employment opportunities in rural communities.

● Entrepreneurship and Local Enterprise: By providing financial services, healthcare, and markets for local products, these cooperatives support local enterprises and entrepreneurship.

- Skill Enhancement: They often provide training and development programs to their members, improving their skills and employment prospects.

Conclusion, Rural cooperatives are essential for creating jobs and supporting economic development in rural areas. Through training and skill development programs, they enhance the capabilities and employment prospects of their members and employees. By fostering local enterprise and entrepreneurship, these cooperatives contribute significantly to the economic vitality and sustainability of rural communities.

2. Urban Employment and Cooperatives

In urban areas, worker cooperatives, housing cooperatives, and consumer cooperatives are significant drivers of employment and equitable economic development. These cooperatives operate across various sectors, such as manufacturing, retail, and services, providing diverse job opportunities and supporting urban economic growth.

- **Worker Cooperatives**

Worker cooperatives are enterprises owned and self-managed by their workers. They empower employees by giving them ownership stakes and decision-making power, which leads to several benefits:

- Enhanced Skills and Professionalism: Members often receive training and opportunities to develop new skills, which enhance their professional growth and job performance.
- Job Satisfaction and Productivity: The sense of ownership and participation in decision-making processes increases job satisfaction and productivity among members.

- Employment Opportunities: By operating in sectors like manufacturing, retail, and services, worker cooperatives create diverse job opportunities that cater to various skill levels and professional backgrounds.

- **Housing Cooperatives**

Housing cooperatives play a vital role in providing affordable housing options for urban residents in today's U.S. community. These cooperatives are owned and managed by the residents themselves, which promotes a sense of community and shared responsibility. The benefits of housing cooperatives include:

- Affordable Housing: Housing cooperatives have been proven that they have made housing more affordable, reducing the cost burden on residents and contributing to economic stability in today's US Economy. By pooling resources and sharing costs, members can access quality housing at lower prices compared to the for-profit private market.
- Community Engagement: Many residents actively participate in the management and maintenance of their homes, fostering a strong sense of community and collaboration. This engagement promotes social cohesion and empowers residents to have a direct say in their living conditions.
- Safe Living Environment: By bundling and mobilizing internal and external resources, housing cooperatives invest in environmental and security improvements. These initiatives include creating community recreational centers, kindergartens, libraries, and other amenities that enhance the quality of life for residents. This collaborative effort not only makes the area safer but also enriches the community with shared spaces and services that benefit everyone.

- **Consumer Cooperatives**

Consumer cooperatives are owned and operated by their members, who use the cooperative's services or purchase its goods. These cooperatives contribute to urban employment and economic development in several significant ways:

- Retail and Services Employment: Consumer cooperatives create jobs in various sectors, including retail stores, grocery outlets, and service-oriented businesses. By operating member-owned establishments, they provide employment opportunities that support local economies.
- Equitable Economic Development: By focusing on the needs of their members, consumer cooperatives ensure that economic

benefits are distributed more equitably. This approach supports local economies and communities by reinvesting profits back into the cooperative or community, promoting sustainable economic growth.
- Market Gauge and Fair Pricing: Consumer cooperatives serve as a true market gauge by helping consumers access competitive prices for goods and services. They minimize the impact of market monopolies by showing the actual costs to produce or supply goods, which helps to keep prices fair and reasonable. Additionally, they often provide services that may be missing from the market, filling gaps and ensuring that consumers have access to necessary goods and services.

Conclusion, Consumer cooperatives play a crucial role in supporting urban employment and promoting equitable economic development. By creating jobs, ensuring fair distribution of economic benefits, and providing competitive pricing for goods and services, these cooperatives help build stronger, more resilient urban communities. Through their member-focused approach, consumer cooperatives contribute to a more balanced and fair market environment, benefiting both members and the wider community.

Overall, Urban cooperatives, through their various forms, not only create employment opportunities but also promote equitable economic development. They empower individuals by enhancing their skills, increasing job satisfaction, and fostering community engagement. By operating in diverse sectors, cooperatives contribute to the resilience and growth of urban economies, making them vital components of sustainable urban development.

3. Ethical, More Decent and Safer Jobs:

Studies by the International Labour Organization (ILO) and other research bodies have indicated that jobs created by cooperative enterprises tend to be more ethical, decent and safer compared to those in other sectors. This is largely due to their foundational values of prioritizing human service over profit. The cooperative governance model and principles contribute significantly to these positive outcomes:

- Democratic Governance: Cooperatives are governed democratically by their members, which often leads to better working conditions as members have a direct say in decision-making processes that affect their work environment.
- Focus on Member Welfare: Cooperatives prioritize the welfare of their members over profits. This often translates to better benefits, job security, and working conditions for employees.
- Long-Term Stability: Cooperatives are typically focused on long-term sustainability rather than short-term gains. This approach can result in more stable, secure employment and services.
- Community Orientation: Cooperatives are rooted in their communities and often reinvest profits back into the community, leading to broader social and economic benefits that improve the quality of life for workers and their families.

• Ethical Practices: Cooperatives generally adhere to high ethical standards and principles, such as fairness, equity, and transparency, which can contribute to safer and more respectful workplaces.

• Training and Development: Many cooperatives invest in the training and development of their members, leading to skill enhancement and better job performance, which contributes to job satisfaction and safety.

4. Boost Government Tax Revenue:

• Cooperatives contribute to government revenue increase through broad-based tax income withholding, as they remit dividend withholding tax on patronage dividends received by members as well as withholding tax from worker's income.

In summary, cooperative enterprises remain integral to the U.S. economy today. They continue to modernize agriculture, expand access to electricity, and improve living standards in rural areas. Credit unions and mutual insurance services enhance access to finance, promoting financial inclusion and security. Cooperatives create employment opportunities in both rural and urban areas, contributing to economic resilience and community development. Their ongoing significance underscores the value of cooperative principles in addressing contemporary economic and social challenges.

VII. Overall Impact

COOPERATIVE ENTERPRISES AS CATALYSTS AND A SPRINGBOARD FOR U.S. ECONOMIC GROWTH

Cooperative enterprises have significantly influenced the U.S. economy throughout history, serving as catalysts for economic growth, community development, equitable resource distribution, true Market Gauge and Fair Pricing. From their early roots in the 19th century to their current role in US modern society, cooperatives have demonstrated resilience and effectiveness in addressing economic challenges and promoting sustainable development across economic sectors.

Promotion of True Community Economic Development

1. Economic Self-Reliance: Cooperatives empower individuals and communities to take control of their economic destinies by pooling resources, sharing risks, and collectively making decisions. By operating on a member-owned and democratic basis, cooperatives promote economic self-reliance and reduce dependency on external economic forces. This self-reliance fosters entrepreneurial spirit and local economic resilience, particularly in rural and underserved communities.

2. Community Development: Cooperatives play a pivotal role in fostering vibrant and cohesive communities. They contribute to community development by providing essential services such as healthcare, education, and housing. Cooperatives often reinvest profits into community projects and initiatives, supporting local infrastructure development and improving overall quality of life. Through community engagement and cooperative principles, these enterprises build social capital and strengthen community bonds.

3. Equitable Resource Access: Cooperatives promote equitable access to resources and opportunities for their members. By

operating on principles of inclusivity and fairness, cooperatives ensure that benefits are distributed fairly among members, regardless of their financial status or background. This inclusive approach helps bridge socioeconomic gaps and promote economic equity, empowering marginalized groups and enhancing social mobility.

Key sectors influenced by cooperatives

1. Agriculture: Agricultural cooperatives have been instrumental in modernizing farming practices, improving productivity, and enhancing market access for farmers. By enabling collective bargaining power and shared resources, agricultural cooperatives ensure that farmers can compete effectively in global markets while maintaining sustainable agricultural practices.

2. Finance: Credit unions and mutual insurance companies provide accessible and affordable financial services to millions of Americans. These cooperatives prioritize member needs over profit, offering lower fees, competitive interest rates, and personalized financial advice. Credit unions promote financial inclusion by serving underserved communities and providing vital credit and savings opportunities.

3. Housing: Housing cooperatives offer affordable and stable housing options through member ownership and collective management. These cooperatives enable residents to have a voice in decision-making and ensure that housing remains affordable and well-maintained. Housing cooperatives play a critical role in addressing housing shortages, promoting community stability, and fostering neighborhood revitalization.

4. Retail: Consumer cooperatives operate retail stores and supply chains that prioritize member needs and community well-being. These cooperatives offer quality products at competitive prices while promoting ethical sourcing and sustainable practices. By supporting local producers and suppliers, consumer cooperatives

contribute to local economic development and environmental sustainability.

5. Utilities: Rural electric cooperatives provide reliable and affordable electricity to rural communities, ensuring access to essential services and supporting economic development. These cooperatives invest in renewable energy projects and infrastructure upgrades, promoting energy efficiency and environmental stewardship. By prioritizing member interests and community needs, rural electric cooperatives enhance quality of life and contribute to sustainable energy solutions.

6. Employment Opportunities: By operating in sectors like manufacturing, retail, and services, worker cooperatives create diverse job opportunities that cater to various skill levels and professional backgrounds.

7. Democratic Governance: Cooperatives are governed democratically by their members, which often leads to better working conditions as members have a direct say in decision-making processes that affect their work environment.

8. Boost Government Tax Revenue: Cooperatives contribute to government revenue through broad-based tax income withholding, remitting dividend withholding tax on patronage dividends received by members, and withholding tax from workers' income.

Conclusion

In conclusion, cooperative enterprises have served as a cornerstone of the U.S. economy by promoting economic self-reliance, fostering community development, and ensuring equitable access to resources. Their impact spans key sectors including agriculture, finance, housing, retail, and utilities, where they continue to innovate, collaborate, and empower individuals and communities. Cooperatives embody principles of cooperation, solidarity, and mutual benefit, making them essential contributors to economic resilience and social progress in the United States and beyond.

VIII. Cooperative Enterprises' Global Foundation initiatives in the U.S

Based on their century-old grassroots practices and achievements, U.S. cooperatives, known for their crucial role in building the domestic economy, have expanded their influence through international cooperative development initiative partnerships to support local cooperatives in Developing and Least Developed Countries (DLDCs). The partnerships initiative, rooted in the cooperative principles of "Cooperation among Cooperatives" and "Concern for Community" aims to share the practical experience of the U.S. cooperative economy as a system in promoting professional cooperatives as community-owned economic organizations to bring sustainable economic development. These initiatives ensure improved agricultural practices, enhanced food security, and fostered economic development in DLDCs worldwide under member control and decision-making principles.

Through these efforts, U.S. cooperatives play a significant role in promoting sustainable community economic development in agricultural practices, access to finance, food security, economic development, and supporting the growth and resilience of cooperatives in the global economy.

Examples of Cooperative Enterprises' Foundations Focused Internationally

1. NCBA CLUSA International

- The National Cooperative Business Association CLUSA International (NCBA CLUSA) launched its international arm in 1953.
- Global Operations: Active in over 20 countries, focusing on agriculture, food security, and economic development.
- Financing: Funded through grants from governments, private donors, and partnerships with other NGOs and international organizations.

- Achievements: Improved agricultural productivity, established market linkages, and promoting women's economic empowerment in DLDCs.
- Challenges and Opportunities: Faces political instability and varying local cooperative laws; opportunities include expanding digital finance solutions and leveraging global cooperative networks.

2. Land O'Lakes International Development

- Land O'Lakes International Development, now known as Land O'Lakes Venture37, was founded in 1981. The nonprofit organization's headquarters is in Arden Hills, Minnesota
- Global Operations: Active in over 80 countries, focusing on agribusiness development, cooperative development, and food security.
- Financing: Supported by USAID, USDA, and other international development funds, as well as corporate partnerships.
- Achievements: Enhanced dairy production, improved market access for farmers, and provided technical assistance for sustainable agriculture in DLDCs.
- Challenges and Opportunities: Challenges include climate change impacts on agriculture and fluctuating commodity prices; opportunities involve scaling innovative agricultural technologies and expanding training programs for farmers.

3. Global Communities (formerly CHF International)

- Global Communities (formerly CHF International) was founded in 1952 as the Cooperative Housing Foundation (CHF).
- Global Operations: Projects across Africa, Asia, Europe, and Latin America, focusing on health, infrastructure, and economic development.

- Financing: Funded by governmental agencies, private sector donations, and international grants.
- Achievements: Built resilient communities through infrastructure projects, promoted public health and supported local economic initiatives in DLDCs.
- Challenges and Opportunities: Faces logistical challenges in conflict zones and regions with poor infrastructure; opportunities include expanding partnerships and adopting innovative community development practices.

4. CHS Inc. Global Impact

- CHS Inc. Global was officially established in 1998 by the merger of Cenex and Harvest States Cooperatives.
- Global Operations: Operates in various countries, focusing on enhancing agricultural productivity, ensuring energy security, and promoting cooperative principles.
- Financing: Funded through CHS Inc.'s revenues, international grants, and partnerships.
- Achievements: Provided essential agricultural inputs, improved grain storage and handling facilities, and promoted sustainable farming practices.
- Challenges and Opportunities: Challenges include navigating complex international trade regulations and addressing climate change impacts; opportunities involve expanding renewable energy projects and enhancing global supply chain efficiencies.

5. Cooperative Development Foundation (CDF)

- The Cooperative Development Foundation (CDF) was established in 1944, originally under the name "Freedom Fund." The organization's initial focus was on helping to rebuild and develop cooperatives in Europe after World War II.
- CDF focused on the reconstruction and development of

European cooperatives in the post-war era, an initiative that engaged the entire U.S. cooperative community.

For example, the CDF created the "Cooperative for American Remittances to Europe."

• Global Operations: Supports projects worldwide, focusing on cooperative development, capacity building, and economic empowerment.

• Financing: Funded through donations, grants, and partnerships with other cooperatives and philanthropic organizations.

• Achievements: Established new cooperatives, provided training and technical assistance, and supported cooperative education initiatives.

• Challenges and Opportunities: Challenges include securing consistent funding and adapting cooperative models to diverse cultural contexts; opportunities involve leveraging digital platforms for cooperative education and expanding partnerships with international NGOs.

6. World Council of Credit Unions (WOCCU) Foundation

• WOCCU Foundation officially began operations on Jan. 1, 1971. Today, WOCCU acts as the leading voice for global advocacy and development on behalf of the international credit union community.

• Global Operations: Works in over 89 countries, focusing on expanding access to financial services, providing technical assistance, and advocating for favorable regulatory environments for credit unions.

• Financing: Funded through contributions from credit unions, grants from governmental and international bodies, and partnerships with financial institutions.

• Achievements: Expanded financial services to underserved communities, improved regulatory frameworks, and enhanced credit union governance and operations in those countries working in.

• Challenges and Opportunities: Challenges include political and economic instability in some regions and varying financial regulations; opportunities include leveraging digital financial technologies, expanding financial literacy programs, and forming strategic alliances to enhance global financial inclusion.

Through these examples, U.S. cooperatives demonstrate their commitment to global cooperative development, leveraging their experience and resources to foster sustainable economic growth and resilience in communities worldwide.

WHY U.S. COOPERATIVES TOOK THE INITIATIVE TO ESTABLISH THESE FOUNDATIONS

U.S. cooperatives recognized the potential of cooperative enterprises to address global challenges and foster sustainable economic development for a broader majority. By leveraging their successful domestic models, they sought to extend their impact worldwide through the establishment of U.S.-based, cooperative-owned foundations. These initiatives aimed to share their practical experience in promoting professional cooperatives as community-owned economic organizations, promoting cooperative economics globally through international cooperative development initiative partnerships. Rooted in the cooperative principles of "Cooperation among Cooperatives" and "Concern for Community," these initiatives aimed to foster cooperative-based sustainable economic development globally in DLDCS.

Key Motivations:

• Promoting Economic Self-Reliance: U.S. cooperatives aimed to extend cooperative models to help communities develop sustainable economic practices by establishing member-owned cooperatives. By sharing their experiences, they empowered communities to build cooperatives based on economic resilience and self-reliance through member-owned cooperative enterprises.

- Enhancing Food Security: U.S. cooperatives recognized the importance of addressing global hunger through improved agricultural methods. By promoting sustainable farming practices and providing access to resources, they aimed to enhance food security and reduce poverty in developing regions through member-owned cooperative enterprises.

- Supporting Community Development: Building Resilient and Self-Sufficient Communities Worldwide was a fundamental goal. U.S. cooperatives sought to create a positive social and economic impact by supporting local cooperatives based on economic development initiatives that improved living standards and provided essential services.

- Expanding Cooperative Networks: Strengthening international cooperative ties and sharing best practices are essential for the growth and development of the cooperative movement globally. U.S. cooperatives aim to build a robust network of cooperatives that can collaborate, innovate, and support one another in achieving common goals.

Principles Guiding the Initiatives:

- Cooperation among Cooperatives: U.S. cooperatives embraced the principle of working together to support the cooperative movement worldwide. By forming partnerships and collaborating with international cooperatives' foundations, they aimed to create a global cooperative network that shared knowledge, resources, and expertise.

- Concern for Community: The principle of prioritizing community well-being drove U.S. cooperatives to take action on a global scale. They aimed to promote social and economic development that was sustainable and inclusive, ensuring that communities could thrive and prosper.

By establishing these foundations, U.S. cooperatives sought to address critical issues such as poverty, food insecurity, and economic instability while fostering the growth and resilience of cooperatives globally. Their initiatives were designed to create lasting positive impacts, leveraging the cooperative model to build a more equitable and sustainable world through cooperative-based economic development.

How these Cooperative Foundations Operate Globally
The Foundation's Operational Strategies and Operate by:

- Collaborating with Local Cooperatives: These foundations partner with local cooperative apex organizations in DLDCs to implement projects tailored to community needs. This collaboration ensures that initiatives are relevant, culturally sensitive, and address the specific challenges faced by local communities.
- Providing Technical Assistance: They offer training, share practical experiences, and provide expertise in areas such as agriculture, finance, cooperative and governance management, and cooperative internal-external capital formation and investment. This support helps local cooperatives in DLDCs enhance their operations and achieve sustainable growth.
- Facilitating Access to Markets: The foundations assist cooperatives in finding and accessing both local and international markets. By creating market linkages, they help local cooperatives in DLDCs improve their profitability and economic stability.
- Training and Capacity Building: Education is a critical component of their work. They focus on educating cooperative members, elected leaders, and professional management on cooperative principles, governance, member engagement, business management, internal-external capital formation and investment, and sustainable practices. This training helps build strong, well-managed local cooperatives in DLDCs that are capable of long-term success.

Collaborating with Local Cooperatives:

● Providing Technical Assistance: Providing practical training, sharing experiences, and offering expertise in agriculture, finance, and cooperative management.

● Facilitating Access to Markets: Helping cooperatives find and access local and international markets.

● Training and Capacity Building: Educating members, elected leaders, and hired professional management on cooperative principles, cooperative governance, member engagement, business management, and sustainable cooperative practices.

The cooperative foundations finance their activities through:

● Grants and Donations: These foundations secure funds from U.S. cooperatives, government agencies, international bodies, and private donors. This financial support is crucial for implementing their global initiatives.

● Partnerships: Collaborating with other NGOs, corporations, and international organizations allows these foundations to pool resources and expertise, enhancing the impact of their projects.

● Revenue-Generating Activities: Some foundations engage in activities that generate income to fund their projects, ensuring financial sustainability.

Achievements:

● Enhanced Agricultural Productivity: By improving farming practices and increasing yields, these foundations help boost food production and improve food security.

● Economic Empowerment: They provide economic opportunities and market access for small-scale farmers and entrepreneurs, fostering local economic development.

- Community Resilience: These foundations build infrastructure and support community development projects, enhancing the overall resilience and well-being of the communities they serve.
- Promoted Cooperative Growth: They help establish and strengthen cooperatives in various sectors, contributing to the growth of the global cooperative movement.

Challenges and Opportunities:
Challenges:

- Political Instability: Operating in regions with political instability can pose significant risks and hinder project implementation.
- Cultural Attitudes: Navigating different cultural attitudes toward cooperatives can be challenging, requiring tailored approaches to gain community acceptance.
- Resource Constraints: Limited resources can restrict the scale and scope of projects, impacting their overall effectiveness.

Opportunities:

- Technological Advancements: Utilizing new technologies can improve agricultural practices, cooperative management, and overall project efficiency.
- Expanding Networks: Building and expanding networks and collaborations with international organizations can enhance resource availability and project impact.
- Scaling Successful Models: Replicating successful cooperative models in new regions can broaden the reach and impact of these foundations.

Conclusion, the international foundations established by U.S. cooperatives demonstrate the power of cooperative economics to address global challenges. By promoting sustainable agricultural practices, enhancing food security, and fostering economic development, these foundations support the growth and resilience of cooperatives worldwide. Their efforts create lasting positive impacts in the communities they serve, showcasing the potential of cooperatives as strategic tools for community economic development on a global scale.

IX. Conclusion

Throughout history and into the present day, cooperative enterprises have played a pivotal role in shaping the U.S. economy and society. From their humble beginnings in the late 19th century to their current impact across diverse sectors, cooperatives have consistently demonstrated their capacity to drive sustainable economic development and enhance community well-being.

- **Recap of the historical and ongoing role of cooperatives**

Since its inception, cooperatives such as the Grange and Farmers' Alliance have empowered farmers by enabling them to pool resources, reduce costs, and gain control over market prices. During the Great Depression, cooperatives surged in importance, providing essential services and economic stability during a period of profound hardship. The New Deal policies further supported their growth, recognizing their potential to foster economic recovery and community resilience.

Post-World War II, cooperatives continued to thrive, modernizing agriculture, expanding access to electricity, and promoting sustainable living standards. Today, cooperatives remain integral to the U.S. economy, enhancing access to finance through credit unions and mutual insurance services, creating employment opportunities in rural and urban areas, and promoting economic self-reliance and equitable resource distribution across various sectors.

- **Final thoughts on the importance of cooperatives in fostering sustainable economic development and community well-being**

Cooperative enterprises embody principles of cooperation, solidarity, and member ownership, which are essential for achieving sustainable economic development and fostering inclusive growth. By prioritizing community needs over profit and promoting democratic governance, cooperatives empower individuals and communities to address local challenges collectively.

The cooperative model not only supports economic resilience but also contributes to social cohesion and community vitality. Through their commitment to ethical business practices, environmental sustainability, and social responsibility, cooperatives play a critical role in building resilient communities and promoting a more equitable society.

In conclusion, the historical and ongoing impact of cooperative enterprises underscores their enduring relevance in shaping a sustainable and prosperous future. As we navigate the challenges of the 21st century, cooperatives stand as exemplars of economic innovation, social responsibility, and community solidarity, continuing to pave the way toward a more inclusive and resilient economy for all.

KEY CHALLENGES OF COOPERATIVE ENTERPRISES AS ORGANIZATION

Cooperatives are Not Well Recognized by the General Public due to

Despite the significant contributions of cooperatives to the U.S. economy at all historical economic stages, they remain poorly recognized, and understood, and receive limited attention from today's policymakers, civil society, Research and study institutions, and even some development institutions. This gap in recognition and understanding can be attributed to several factors, including the limited capacity of cooperatives to sensitize local partners and citizens. Here are some key points to consider:

1. Lack of Awareness and Education:

- Educational Curricula: the cooperative model is not widely taught or promoted in educational curricula. Many people are unfamiliar with the principles and benefits of cooperatives due to a lack of exposure and understanding.

● Integration in Education: Educational institutions should integrate cooperative studies into their programs to increase awareness and understanding among future leaders and professionals.

2. Media Coverage:

● Underrepresentation: Cooperatives often receive less media coverage compared to traditional corporate businesses. Major media outlets tend to focus on larger, profit-driven corporations, leaving cooperatives underrepresented in mainstream narratives.

● Media Campaigns: Increased media campaigns and partnerships with journalists can help highlight the successes and benefits of cooperatives.

3. Misconceptions and Stereotypes:

● Common Misconceptions: there are misconceptions that cooperatives are small-scale, less efficient, or only relevant in certain sectors like agriculture. These stereotypes can deter public interest and engagement.

● Public Awareness Initiatives: Public awareness initiatives, workshops, and seminars can help dispel these myths and educate the public on the diverse roles cooperatives play in the economy.

4. Visibility and Branding:

● Marketing Challenges: Cooperatives may not have the same level of visibility and branding as large corporations. They often lack the marketing budgets and strategies that help traditional businesses achieve widespread recognition.

● Strategic Marketing: Enhancing the visibility and branding of cooperatives through strategic marketing and public relations efforts can help change this perception.

5. Few Universities Have Cooperative Studies as a Curriculum in the U.S.:

• Limited Academic Exposure: The cooperative model is not commonly included in university curricula. This limits academic exposure, research on cooperative gaps and solutions, and the development of specialized knowledge and skills related to cooperatives.

• Development of Specialized Courses: Universities should develop specialized courses and programs focused on cooperative studies to foster a deeper understanding and appreciation of the cooperative model.

6. Lack of Research and Product Development:

• Insufficient Research: There is often insufficient research on cooperatives and a lack of investment in product development tailored to the cooperative model.

• National-Level Apex Cooperatives: The lack of strong national-level apex cooperatives focused on research, product development, and community awareness limits the potential growth and innovation within the sector.

• Partnerships with Academic Institutions: Establishing partnerships between cooperatives and academic institutions can foster innovation and provide a comprehensive analysis of cooperative economic impacts.

THE ROLE OF RESEARCH AND ACADEMIC INSTITUTIONS

National university researchers and research programs play a crucial role in conducting comprehensive and in-depth analyses of the socio-economic impacts of cooperatives. This research can provide a longitudinal perspective on the cooperative business model, highlighting its immense socio-economic contributions and presenting evidence-based information to policymakers to enhance cooperative advocacy. However, the cooperative sector must actively invest in and engage with researchers and academic institutions to facilitate this process. Here are some steps that can be taken:

1. Engage Academic Institutions
Collaborative Research Projects:

- Proposal Submission: Cooperatives should reach out to universities and research institutions to propose collaborative research projects focused on the socio-economic impacts of cooperatives.
- Research Funding: Seek funding and support for these research projects from development organizations and cooperative networks.
- Dedicated Departments: Advocate for the establishment of departments focused on cooperative studies within business and economics colleges and universities.

2. Promote Comprehensive Research
In-Depth Studies:

- Encouragement: Encourage researchers to conduct in-depth studies that capture the heterogeneous and diverse nature of the cooperative sector.

● Detailed Analysis: Aim to provide a detailed analysis of the national socio-economic impacts of cooperatives, highlighting their role in building self-help communities and competitive market economies.

3. Mass-Based Awareness Campaigns
Education and Advocacy:

● Awareness Campaigns: Engage at both institutional and community levels to educate the public, policymakers, and development institutions about the role and benefits of cooperatives.

● School Partnerships: Cooperatives can work closely with school districts and counties by sponsoring student field trips and school feeding programs in collaboration with Cooperative Educational Service Agencies (CESAs) and The Urban School Food Alliance.

● Highlight Advantages: Focus on the unique advantages of the cooperative model, such as democratic governance, community focus, and economic resilience.

● Stakeholder Engagement: Use workshops, seminars, and public lectures to inform different stakeholders about the importance of cooperatives in promoting sustainable economic growth and community development.

Leveraging Media Platforms:

● Media Utilization: Use social media, television, radio, and print media to disseminate information about cooperatives.

● Public Events: Host fairs, exhibitions, and community festivals to showcase success stories and impacts of cooperatives.

● Educational Programs: Create educational materials, such as documentaries, infographics, and online courses, to reach a wider audience and deepen understanding of the cooperative model.

● Sponsored Media Programs: Cooperatives should sponsor well-known media programs to enhance visibility and credibility.

Using Products as Mass-Based Awareness Campaign Tools:

- Product Engagement: Cooperatives like Land O'Lakes Inc. and Sunkist Growers, Inc. can directly engage with consumers through their products.
- Interactive Marketing: Implement strategies such as product packaging that includes information about cooperatives and their benefits.
- Consumer Activities: Host activities like taste testing events, farm tours, and workshops where consumers can learn about the cooperative's values and practices.
- Retail Collaboration: Create in-store displays and promotions that educate consumers about the cooperative model and its positive impact on communities.

By addressing these gaps and actively promoting the cooperative model, cooperatives can gain greater recognition and support from the general public, policymakers, and development institutions. This increased awareness and understanding can help cooperatives continue to thrive and contribute to sustainable economic development and community well-being.

WHY DO TODAY'S US POLICYMAKERS GIVE LESS ATTENTION TO COOPERATIVES THAN IN THE EARLY 20TH CENTURY?

Despite their potential to enhance free markets, privatization, and deregulation by being community-owned and locally managed, cooperatives do not receive the same level of support from U.S. policymakers today as they did in the 19th and early 20th centuries. This lack of support persists even though cooperatives like Sunkist Growers, Inc., Land O'Lakes, Inc., CHS Inc., Global Communities (formerly CHF International), and the National Rural Electric Cooperative Association (NRECA), as well as international examples like Mondragon, Crédit

Agricole, and Rabobank, have proven to be efficient and capable of driving economic growth and returning surplus profits to their communities and members.

In addition, during the recent financial crisis, while large corporations and private banks requested government bailouts, cooperatives survived on their own, demonstrating their efficiency and capability to drive sustainable economic growth. Despite this demonstrated resilience and efficiency, cooperatives still face a lack of support from policymakers. Several factors contribute to this discrepancy in support:

1. Shift in Economic Ideology:

- Neoliberal Policies: Since the mid-20th century, there has been a shift towards neoliberal economic policies that prioritize large-scale, profit-driven businesses over collective, community-focused enterprises like cooperatives. This ideology often views cooperatives as less compatible with free-market principles, despite the evidence of Sunkist Growers, Inc., Land O'Lakes, Inc., CHS Inc., Global Communities (CHF International), the National Rural Electric Cooperative Association (NRECA), as well Mondragon, Crédit Agricole, and Rabobank to the contrary.
- Focus on Large Corporations: Policymakers often believe that large corporations are more capable of driving economic growth and innovation compared to smaller, locally managed cooperatives.

2. Influence of Large Corporations:

- Lobbying Power: Large corporations have substantial financial resources to influence policymaking through lobbying, campaign contributions, and other means. Cooperatives, with fewer financial resources, struggle to match this influence.

• Corporate Dominance: The dominance of large corporations in the economy translates into significant political power, which they use to advocate for policies that favor their interests over those of cooperatives.

3. Regulatory and Legal Challenges:

• Complex Regulations: Cooperatives often face complex regulatory environments that can be burdensome and costly to navigate. These regulations are typically designed with traditional business models in mind, making it difficult for cooperatives to comply.

• Lack of Cooperative-Friendly Policies: There is a lack of specific policies that support the unique structure and needs of cooperatives, unlike the earlier period when there was more legislative support for cooperative models.

4. Perception and Awareness Issues:

• Lack of Understanding: There is often a lack of understanding among policymakers about how cooperatives function and their potential benefits. This can lead to a preference for more familiar corporate models.

• Perceived Inefficiency: Some policymakers perceive cooperatives as less efficient or innovative compared to traditional businesses, despite evidence to the contrary.

5. Historical Context and Economic Priorities:

• Different Economic Contexts: In the 19th and early 20th centuries, cooperatives were seen as a solution to various economic challenges, including those faced by farmers and workers. Today's economic context, with its focus on globalization and technological advancement, prioritizes different types of solutions.

● Focus on Short-Term Gains: Policymakers often prioritize short-term economic gains and immediate job creation over long-term, sustainable economic models like cooperatives.

6. Fragmentation and Representation:

● Fragmented Cooperative Movement: The cooperative movement today is more fragmented and less unified compared to the past, making it harder to advocate effectively for supportive policies.
● Weak Political Representation: Cooperatives generally lack strong political representation compared to other business interests, leading to less influence in policy-making processes.

Addressing the Lack of Support

To gain greater support from policymakers, the cooperative sector can consider the following strategies:

1. Enhance Advocacy and Lobbying Efforts:

● Unified Voice: Form coalitions and alliances to create a unified voice for cooperative advocacy.
● Engage with Policymakers: Actively engage with policymakers to educate them about the benefits and potential of cooperatives.

2. Increase Public Awareness:

● Educational Campaigns: Launch educational campaigns to raise awareness about the cooperative model and its benefits among the public and policymakers.
● Highlight Success Stories: Showcase successful cooperatives and their positive impacts on local economies and communities.

3. Promote Research and Evidence-Based Advocacy:

- Support Research: Invest in research to provide evidence-based information on the socio-economic impacts of cooperatives.
- Collaborate with Academia: Partner with academic institutions to conduct and publish research that highlights the effectiveness of cooperatives.

4. Simplify Regulatory Environments:

- Policy Reforms: Advocate for policy reforms that simplify regulatory requirements and reduce the burden on cooperatives.
- Develop Cooperative-Friendly Policies: Push for the development of policies specifically designed to support the growth and sustainability of cooperatives.

5. Strengthen the Cooperative Movement:

- Build Strong Networks: Strengthen networks and alliances within the cooperative movement to enhance collective advocacy efforts.
- Promote Cooperative Education: Educate cooperative members and leaders on effective advocacy and engagement strategies.

By addressing these challenges and actively promoting the cooperative model, cooperatives can gain greater recognition and support from policymakers, contributing to sustainable economic development and community well-being.

COOPERATIVE ENTERPRISE'S REMARKABLE STABILITY AND RESILIENCE BUSINESS MODEL

The remarkable stability and resilience of cooperative enterprises during the 2008 financial crisis exemplify a robust business model capable of withstanding economic turbulence. While many large corporations and private banks required government bailouts to survive, cooperatives demonstrated their efficiency and capacity to drive sustainable economic growth. This resilience can be attributed to several factors inherent to the cooperative model:

1. Member-Centric Focus

- **Prudent Financial Management**: Cooperatives prioritize the needs and well-being of their members over profit maximization, leading to more cautious financial management and risk-taking.
- **Long-Term Interests**: Financial decisions are made with the long-term interests of the community in mind, ensuring stability and sustained growth.

2. Democratic Governance

- Balanced Decision-Making: The democratic structure of cooperatives ensures that decision-making is more balanced and reflective of the members' interests.
- Fairness and Accountability: Each member typically has one vote, promoting fairness and accountability within the organization and contributing to sustainable business practices.

3. Long-Term Orientation

- Focus on Long-Term Goals: Cooperatives emphasize long-term goals rather than short-term profits, contributing to their stability during economic downturns.
- Avoidance of Risky Behavior: This long-term perspective reduces the likelihood of engaging in risky financial behavior that can lead to crises.

4. Community Integration

- Local Roots: Cooperatives are deeply rooted in their local communities, providing essential services and maintaining close relationships with their member base.
- Steady Support: Community integration offers a steady source of support during crises, as members are more likely to remain loyal and supportive.

Case Studies: Cooperative Resilience During the 2008 Financial Crisis

During the 2008 financial crisis, many cooperatives in various sectors, including credit unions, worker cooperatives, and consumer cooperatives, showed remarkable stability. Examples include:

- Credit Unions: These institutions maintained healthier loan portfolios compared to traditional banks, partly due to their conservative lending practices and focus on member welfare. This stability was evident as credit unions faced fewer defaults and maintained higher levels of liquidity.
- Worker Cooperatives: Many worker cooperatives avoided massive layoffs and instead implemented shared work hours and wage adjustments to weather the economic storm. This approach preserved jobs and maintained member incomes.
- Consumer Cooperatives: These organizations continued to provide essential goods and services to their communities, often at more stable prices than for-profit competitors, thereby supporting local economies during the downturn.

Recognizing Limitations and Future Directions

It is also important to acknowledge that while cooperatives displayed resilience, they were not entirely immune to the crisis's effects. The degree of impact varied depending on the sector and the specific cooperative's circumstances. Nonetheless, the overall performance of cooperatives during the financial crisis has been cited as a testament to their efficiency and capability to contribute to sustainable economic growth.

Strategies to Enhance Cooperative Resilience

To further enhance the resilience and stability of cooperatives, the following strategies can be considered:

1. Strengthen Financial Education: Promote financial literacy among cooperative members to ensure informed decision-making.
2. Diversify Income Sources: Encourage cooperatives to diversify their income sources to reduce dependency on a single revenue stream.
3. Enhance Collaboration: Foster collaboration among cooperatives to share resources, knowledge, and best practices.
4. Invest in Technology: Adopt advanced technologies to improve operational efficiency and member services.
5. Policy Advocacy: Advocate for supportive policies that recognize the unique structure and benefits of cooperatives, reduce regulatory burdens, and enhance access to funding.

By leveraging these strategies, cooperatives can continue to demonstrate their resilience and stability, driving sustainable economic growth and supporting community well-being, even in challenging economic environments.

During the 2008 financial crisis, many cooperatives in various sectors, including credit unions, worker cooperatives, and consumer cooperatives, showed remarkable stability. For example, credit unions often maintained healthier loan portfolios compared to traditional banks, partly due to their conservative lending practices and focus on member welfare.

However, it is also important to acknowledge that while cooperatives displayed resilience, they were not entirely immune to the crisis's effects. The degree of impact varied depending on the sector and the specific cooperative's circumstances. Nonetheless, the overall performance of cooperatives during the financial crisis has been cited as a testament to their efficiency and capability to contribute to sustainable economic growth.

AFRICA IS NOT LEARNING FROM THE COOPERATIVE MODEL

Though the cooperative movement in the U.S. was shaped by specific historical contexts, Africa's current economic situation closely mirrors that of the U.S. during the early 19th and early 20th centuries, a time when cooperatives played a pivotal role in U.S. economic growth and modernization. Despite the clear potential of cooperatives to drive economic development, promote equitable resource distribution, and enhance community resilience, Africa has yet to fully embrace this model. Why isn't Africa learning from the U.S. cooperative model to foster economic change and modernization?

Key Factors Contributing to the Gap

1. Limited Awareness and Understanding:

• Lack of Education: Many African communities and policymakers have limited exposure to the benefits and operations of cooperatives.

● Need for Advocacy: There is a critical need for increased advocacy and education to illustrate how cooperatives can drive economic growth and community development.

2. Weak Institutional and Policy Support:

● Insufficient Policies: Many African countries lack robust policies and regulations that support the development and sustainability of cooperatives.

● Inadequate Infrastructure: The absence of institutional support and necessary infrastructure hampers cooperative activities.

3. Cultural and Social Factors:

● Individualism vs. Collectivism: Cultural norms often prioritize individual entrepreneurship over collective approaches, creating barriers to cooperative models.

● Trust Issues: Social dynamics and historical experiences can undermine the trust and collaboration essential for successful cooperatives.

4. Economic and Structural Challenges:

● Infrastructure Deficiencies: Poor infrastructure and economic instability limit the effectiveness and growth potential of cooperatives.

● Access to Resources: Limited access to markets, finance, and technology constrains the development of cooperatives.

5. Historical Context and Adaptation:

● Contextual Differences: Direct replication of the US cooperative model may not address Africa's unique historical, cultural, and economic contexts.

● Learning from Local Successes: Africa needs to adapt cooperative principles to fit local conditions, drawing from both international experiences and successful local models.

Steps Forward for Africa

1. Promote Awareness and Education:

● Implement educational initiatives and advocacy campaigns to highlight the benefits and successes of cooperatives.

2. Strengthen Institutional Support:

● Develop supportive policies and create infrastructure to facilitate cooperative development.

3. Foster a Cooperative Culture:

Encourage collaboration and trust-building within communities to support cooperative endeavors.

4. Address Economic Barriers:

● Invest in infrastructure and provide better access to finance and markets for cooperatives.

5. Adapt the Model:

● Customize cooperative models to fit Africa's specific socio-economic contexts, leveraging both local and international best practices.

Additional Considerations

1. Historical and Structural Challenges:

● Many African countries face structural challenges such as political instability and weak institutions, complicating the adoption and scaling of cooperative models.

2. Policy Environment:

● The policy environment often favors large-scale, foreign-owned enterprises, with insufficient support for cooperative development.

3. Lack of Awareness and Education:

● Limited integration of cooperative principles into national education systems and development strategies hinders widespread understanding.

4. Economic Conditions:

● High levels of poverty and economic inequality can make it challenging to establish and sustain cooperatives, as people may prioritize immediate economic survival.

5. International Influence:

● Economic policies influenced by international financial institutions and donor countries may prioritize traditional capitalist models over cooperative economics.

Strategies to Enhance Recognition and Support for Cooperatives

1. Education and Awareness Campaigns:

● Integrate cooperative principles into educational curricula and conduct public awareness campaigns.

2. Policy Reforms:

● Advocate for supportive policies such as tax incentives, access to financing, and regulatory frameworks tailored to cooperatives.

3. Media and Visibility:

● Encourage media coverage of successful cooperatives and use social media to increase visibility.

4. Capacity Building:

● Provide training and resources to cooperative members and leaders for better management, governance, and advocacy.

5. International Collaboration:

● Foster global cooperation to share best practices and support cooperative growth in Africa.

6. Community Engagement:

● Engage local communities in the formation and management of cooperatives to ensure they meet local needs and gain community support.

7. Use IT & Information Management System:

- Enhance Service Efficiency by Implementing IT and information management systems to improve the efficiency of cooperative services, leading to greater member satisfaction and attracting new members

By addressing these challenges and implementing targeted strategies, Africa can enhance the recognition and support for cooperatives, potentially unlocking significant economic and social benefits, and fostering sustainable development and modernization.

X. References

1. ACE Hardware. History and Facts. Retrieved from acehardware.com.
2. Adams, C. (2001). The Essential Agrarian: The Case for Cooperative Land Management. University of Nebraska Press.
3. Adams, John. "Cooperative Enterprise: Facing the Challenge of Globalization." Cambridge University Press, 2013.
4. A Slice of New York. "About Us." A Slice of New York. Retrieved from [URL] (n.d.).
5. Bassett, S. (2015). Cooperative Movement in the United States. In T. Stanton (Ed.), Encyclopedia of American Social Movements. Routledge.
6. Birchall, J. (2013). People-Centred Businesses: Co-operatives, Mutuals and the Idea of Membership. Palgrave Macmillan.
7. Birchall, Johnston. "Co-operative Principles Then and Now." International Labour Organization, 2012.
8. Birchall, Johnston, and Lou Hammond Ketilson. "Resilience of the Cooperative Business Model in Times of Crisis." International Labour Organization, 2009.
9. Cheney, George. "Values at Work: Employee Participation Meets Market Pressure at Mondragon." Cornell University Press, 1999.
10. Cook, M. L. (1995). The Future of U.S. Agricultural Cooperatives: A Neo-Institutional Approach. University of Wisconsin Press.
11. Cronon, William. "Nature's Metropolis: Chicago and the Great West." W. W. Norton & Company, 1991.
12. Dawson, P. (2018). Cooperatives in Agriculture: Case Studies from the United States and Europe. CABI.
13. Deller, Steven C., et al. "Measuring the Economic Impact of Cooperatives." University of Wisconsin Center for Cooperatives, 2009.
14. Deller, Steven C., et al. "Measuring the Economic Impact of Cooperatives." University of Wisconsin Center for Cooperatives, 2017.
15. Equal Exchange. "About Us." Equal Exchange, n.d.
16. Fairbairn, Brett. "The Meaning of Rochdale: The Rochdale Pioneers and the Co-operative Principles." Centre for the Study of Co-operatives, University of Saskatchewan, 1994.
17. Farm Credit Administration. (2023). History of the Farm Credit System. Retrieved from FCA.gov.
18. Gordon Nembhard, Jessica. "Collective Courage: A History of African American Cooperative Economic Thought and Practice." Penn State University Press, 2014.
19. Greenberg, Edward S. "Workers' Self-Management in the United States." Temple University Press, 1986.
20. Hendrikse, G. W. J., & Bijman, J. (Eds.). (2002). Cooperation in Agriculture: The Evolution of Farmers' Cooperatives. Wageningen Academic Publishers.

21. Hoyt, David P. "The Co-operative Movement in the United States." Cornell University Press, 1951.

22. International Co-operative Alliance. "Cooperative Identity, Values & Principles." ICA, 2020.

23. International Co-operative Alliance (ICA). "Blueprint for a Co-operative Decade." ICA, 2013.

24. Isthmus Engineering. "About Us." Isthmus Engineering, n.d.

25. Kawano, Emily. Building Co-operative Power: Stories and Strategies from Worker Co-operatives in the Connecticut River Valley. Levellers Press, 2013.

26. Mujeres Unidas. "About Us." Mujeres Unidas, n.d.

27. National Cooperative Bank. (2023). NCB Annual Report 2023. Retrieved from NCB.coop.

28. National Cooperative Business Association. (2019). Cooperatives: Principles and Practices in the 21st Century Economy. Retrieved from https://ncba.coop/cooperatives-principles-and-practices.

29. National Cooperative Business Association. (2020). Cooperatives Impact Report: The Economic and Social Contributions of America's Cooperatives. Retrieved from https://ncba.coop/impactreport.

30. National Credit Union Administration (NCUA). History of St. Mary's Bank Credit Union. Retrieved from NCUA.gov.

31. National Grange. "About Us." The National Grange of the Order of Patrons of Husbandry, 2023.

32. National Rural Electric Cooperative Association (NRECA). (2020). The Power of Cooperatives: The Cooperative Difference in Action. Retrieved from https://www.cooperative.com/public/pages/default.aspx.

33. NCUA. "Credit Union Data." National Credit Union Administration, 2024.

34. Navy Federal Credit Union Annual Report, (2023). Retrieved from https://www.navyfederal.org/content/dam/nfculibs/pdfs/membership/2023-Annual-Report.pdf.

35. Paris, T. (2019). The Role of Cooperatives in Rural Development. Journal of Agricultural Cooperation, 47(2), 81-96.

36. Roelant's, Bruno, Hyungsik Eum, Simel Esim, Sonja Novkovic, and Willi Savall. "Cooperatives and Employment: A Global Report." CICOPA, 2014.

37. Roosevelt, F. D. (1937). Address on the Purposes and Foundations of the Recovery Program. Retrieved from https://www.presidency.ucsb.edu/documents/address-the-purposes-and-foundations-the-recovery-program.

38. Roosevelt, Franklin D. "Public Papers of the Presidents of the United States: Franklin D. Roosevelt, 1933." U.S. Government Printing Office, 1938.

39. Rural Electrification Act, 1936. Retrieved from USDA Rural Development.

40. Shaffer, Beverly R. Cooperative Housing in Washington, D.C.: A Brief History. U.S. Department of Housing and Urban Development, 2006.

41. United Nations. (2002). Cooperatives in Social Development: Report of the Secretary-General. Retrieved from https://www.un.org/esa/socdev/publications/coopdevstudy.pdf.

42. United States Department of Agriculture (USDA). (2020). Research on Cooperative Development. Retrieved from https://www.rd.usda.gov/publications/research-cooperative-development.

43. Whyte, William Foote, and Kathleen King Whyte. "Making Mondragon: The Growth and Dynamics of the Worker Cooperative Complex." ILR Press, 1991.

SUPPLEMENTARY TOPIC EXPLANATIONS

Cooperative grain elevator stores, and Storage Receipt uses

Cooperative grain elevator stores play a crucial role in helping farmers access finance by using grain elevator store receipts as loan guarantees. Here's how this process typically works:

1. Storage of Grain

- Farmers Store Grain: Farmers bring their harvested grain to a cooperative grain elevator for storage. The grain elevator safely stores the grain and issues a receipt to the farmer.
- Grain Elevator Receipt: This receipt details the quantity, quality, and type of grain stored. It acts as proof of the farmer's assets held at the elevator.

2. Issuance of Warehouse Receipts

- Documentation: The cooperative grain elevator issues a warehouse receipt or store receipt, which is a legal document acknowledging the storage of grain.
- Negotiable Instrument: These receipts are often considered "negotiable instruments," meaning they can be transferred to another party, such as a bank or financial institution, as collateral.

3. Accessing Finance

- Collateral for Loans: Farmers can use the grain elevator store receipts as collateral to obtain loans from banks or other lending institutions.
- Loan Application: When applying for a loan, the farmer presents the grain elevator receipt to the lender as a guarantee of the value of the stored grain.

4. Valuation and Loan Approval

- Valuation of Grain: The lender assesses the value of the grain based on the details in the receipt, considering current market prices and the quality of the grain.
- Loan Terms: Based on the valuation, the lender determines the loan amount, interest rate, and repayment terms. The loan amount is typically a percentage of the grain's market value.

5. Loan Disbursement

- Funds for Farmers: Once the loan is approved, the lender disburses the funds to the farmer, who can then use the money for various needs, such as purchasing seeds, fertilizers, equipment, or covering operational costs.
- Loan Repayment: The farmer agrees to repay the loan according to the terms set by the lender. The grain stored in the elevator acts as security for the loan.

6. Grain Sale and Loan Repayment

- Selling the Grain: When market conditions are favorable, or when the loan is due, the farmer can sell the grain stored at the elevator.

- Settlement: The proceeds from the grain sale are used to repay the loan. If the grain is sold for more than the loan amount, the farmer retains the surplus. If the sale proceeds are insufficient, the farmer is responsible for covering the remaining loan balance.

Benefits of Using Grain Elevator Receipts for Finance

- Access to Capital: Enables farmers to access needed funds without having to sell their grain immediately, allowing them to wait for better market prices.
- Reduced Risk: Provides a secure way to borrow money, as the grain acts as collateral, reducing the lender's risk.
- Improved Cash Flow: Helps farmers manage cash flow more effectively, ensuring they have the resources needed for planting, harvesting, and other operations.
- Strengthened Bargaining Position: Farmers are not forced to sell their grain at low prices immediately after harvest; they can wait for higher prices, improving their bargaining position.

Cooperative grain elevator stores, therefore, provide a vital service by enabling farmers to leverage their stored grain to access much-needed financing, enhancing their financial stability and operational flexibility.

THE MONDRAGON COOPERATIVE OF SPAIN

The Mondragon Corporation in Spain is one of the world's largest and most successful examples of a worker cooperative. Here is a detailed explanation of what Mondragon does for its members and what its members do for the cooperative:

What Mondragon Does for Its Members:

- Ownership and Participation: Members of Mondragon are not just employees; they are co-owners of the cooperative. This gives them a direct stake in the success of the business and the right to participate in decision-making processes. Each member typically has one vote, ensuring democratic governance.
- Profit Sharing: Profits generated by the cooperative are distributed among members. This can come in the form of dividends or allocations to individual capital accounts, enhancing members' financial well-being.
- Job Security and Stability: Mondragon prioritizes job security for its members. In times of economic difficulty, the cooperative makes efforts to redistribute workers across different units within the corporation to avoid layoffs.
- Education and Training: Mondragon invests heavily in the education and training of its members. It runs its own university, Mondragon University, which provides advanced training and education to help members develop skills and advance in their careers.
- Social Services: The cooperative offers a range of social services, including healthcare, pensions, and other benefits, ensuring that members and their families are well cared for.
- Support for Entrepreneurship: Mondragon supports innovation and entrepreneurship among its members. It provides resources and support for members who wish to start new cooperative businesses within the Mondragon framework.

What Members Do for Mondragon:

- Work and Productivity: Members contribute their labor and skills to the cooperative, working in various roles across its diverse business units, which include manufacturing, retail, finance, and education.

- Participation in Governance: Members actively participate in the governance of the cooperative. They attend general assemblies, vote on important decisions, and can be elected to leadership positions.
- Financial Contributions: Members often make initial capital contributions to join the cooperative. These contributions help finance the cooperative's operations and investments.
- Commitment to Values: Members commit to the cooperative values of solidarity, participation, and mutual support. This commitment fosters a strong organizational culture and ensures that the cooperative operates according to its principles.
- Innovation and Improvement: Members are encouraged to contribute ideas and initiatives to improve operations, innovate new products or services, and enhance the cooperative's competitiveness and sustainability.

Summary:

The relationship between Mondragon and its members is highly reciprocal. Mondragon provides members with economic opportunities, job security, education, and a say in governance, while members contribute their labor, participate in decision-making, make financial contributions, and uphold the cooperative's values. This mutual support and collaboration have helped Mondragon become a model of cooperative success and sustainability.

The Dust Bowl

Overview: The Dust Bowl was a period of severe dust storms that greatly damaged the ecology and agriculture of the American and Canadian prairies during the 1930s. It was primarily caused by a combination of drought and poor farming practices that left the soil exposed and vulnerable to wind erosion.

Causes:

- Severe Drought: Prolonged periods of drought left the soil dry and loose.
- Poor Agricultural Practices: Over-plowing and overgrazing destroyed the native grasses that held the soil in place, making it more susceptible to erosion.
- Economic Factors: The demand for wheat during World War I led to increased farming, which further degraded the land.

Impact:

- Environmental: Massive dust storms, known as "black blizzards," swept across the plains, displacing topsoil and making farming nearly impossible.
- Economic: Farmers lost their crops and livelihoods, leading to widespread poverty and displacement.
- Social: Thousands of families, often referred to as "Okies" because many were from Oklahoma, migrated west to California in search of work and better living conditions.

The solutions to the Dust Bowl involved a combination of immediate relief efforts, long-term agricultural practices, and government interventions aimed at restoring the environment and supporting affected communities. Here are the key measures that were taken:

Short-Term Relief
Emergency Relief:

- The government provided direct aid to farmers and families affected by the Dust Bowl. This included food, clothing, and financial assistance.
- The Works Progress Administration (WPA) and other New Deal programs provided jobs to displaced workers, helping to build

infrastructure and restore communities.

Long-Term Agricultural Practices
Soil Conservation Techniques:

- Farmers were educated on new farming techniques that helped prevent soil erosion. This included contour plowing, crop rotation, strip farming, and terracing.
- Planting cover crops such as grasses and legumes helped to hold the soil in place and restore soil fertility.

Shelterbelts:

- The Prairie States Forestry Project, initiated in 1935, involved planting long rows of trees (shelterbelts) to act as windbreaks. These trees helped reduce wind erosion and protected the soil.

Government Interventions
Soil Conservation Service (SCS):

- Established in 1935 under the Department of Agriculture, the SCS (now the Natural Resources Conservation Service) promoted soil conservation practices and worked directly with farmers to implement them.
- The SCS also conducted research and provided technical assistance to improve farming methods and land management.

Resettlement and Rehabilitation Programs:

- The Resettlement Administration (RA) was created to help relocate farm families to more productive lands and to develop cooperative farming communities.

- The Farm Security Administration (FSA) provided loans and grants to farmers for purchasing equipment and improving their land.

Education and Research
Agricultural Extension Services:

- Extension services provided education and resources to farmers about soil conservation techniques and sustainable farming practices.
- Research stations were established to study and develop better agricultural methods.

Environmental Restoration
Grassland Restoration:

- Efforts were made to restore native grasslands by reseeding and protecting them from overgrazing.
- Federal and state agencies worked to restore the natural vegetation that had been depleted.

Legal and Policy Measures
Agricultural Adjustment Act (AAA):

- The AAA aimed to reduce crop surplus and stabilize prices by paying farmers to reduce the production of certain crops. This helped decrease the pressure on the land and allowed for recovery.

Impact of the Solutions

- These measures collectively helped to mitigate the effects of the Dust Bowl and restore the ecological balance of the affected regions. Over time, these efforts led to more sustainable agricultural practices and improved land management, which helped to

prevent the recurrence of such severe dust storms and soil degradation. The lessons learned from the Dust Bowl also influenced future agricultural policies and practices in the United States.

The Great Depression

Overview: The Great Depression was a severe worldwide economic downturn that lasted from 1929 to about 1939. It was the longest, deepest, and most widespread depression of the twentieth century.

Causes:

- Stock Market Crash of 1929: The sudden and dramatic collapse of stock prices on October 29, 1929 (known as "Black Tuesday") triggered a financial panic and loss of confidence in the economy.
- Bank Failures: Many banks failed due to loan defaults and insufficient reserves, leading to the loss of savings for millions of Americans.
- Reduction in Consumer Spending and Investment: With reduced income and confidence, consumer spending and business investment plummeted.
- Global Trade Decline: Protectionist policies, such as the "Smoot-Hawley Tariff," led to a decline in international trade.

Impact:

- Unemployment: Unemployment rates soared, with nearly a quarter of the workforce out of jobs at the peak of the Depression.
- Economic Hardship: Businesses closed, banks failed, and millions of people lost their homes and savings.
- Social and Psychological Effects: The Depression caused significant social and psychological distress, including increased rates of poverty, homelessness, and mental health issues.

- Political Changes: The economic crisis led to significant political changes, including the election of Franklin D. Roosevelt and the implementation of the New Deal, a series of programs and reforms designed to promote economic recovery and social welfare.

The solutions to the Great Depression involved a series of economic reforms, government interventions, and policy changes that aimed to stabilize the economy, provide relief to the unemployed, and prevent future economic crises. These measures are collectively known as the "New Deal," which was implemented by President Franklin D. Roosevelt. Here are the key components of the solutions:

Immediate Relief Efforts
   Emergency Banking Act:

- Closed all banks for a "bank holiday" to prevent further runs and to stabilize the banking system. Only solvent banks were allowed to reopen after being inspected.

Federal Emergency Relief Administration (FERA):

- Provided direct relief and job programs for the unemployed. Distributed funds to state agencies for direct aid to those in need.

Civilian Conservation Corps (CCC):

- Provided jobs for young men in public works projects, such as reforestation, park maintenance, and soil erosion prevention.

Public Works Administration (PWA) and Works Progress Administration (WPA):

- Funded large-scale public works projects to create jobs and improve infrastructure.
- WPA employed millions in various projects, including construction, arts, and education.
- Economic Recovery Measures

Agricultural Adjustment Act (AAA):

- Aimed to raise crop prices by paying farmers to reduce production.
- Addressed overproduction and helped stabilize farm income.

National Industrial Recovery Act (NIRA):

- Established the National Recovery Administration (NRA) to set fair practices and codes for industries.
- Promoted industrial recovery by regulating wages, prices, and working hours.

Tennessee Valley Authority (TVA):

- Created to develop the Tennessee Valley region, providing jobs, electricity, and flood control.
- Built dams and power plants, bringing modernization and economic development to the region.

Financial Reforms
Securities Act of 1933 and Securities Exchange Act of 1934:

- Regulated the stock market and reduced fraudulent activities.
- Established the Securities and Exchange Commission (SEC) to oversee securities markets.

Glass-Steagall Act:

- Separated commercial and investment banking to reduce risks.
- Created the Federal Deposit Insurance Corporation (FDIC) to insure bank deposits and restore confidence in the banking system.
- Social Welfare Programs

Social Security Act of 1935:

- Established a social safety net by providing unemployment insurance, old-age pensions, and aid to disabled and needy individuals.
- Marked the beginning of the modern welfare state in the U.S. Labor Reforms

Wagner Act (National Labor Relations Act):

- Protected workers' rights to unionize and bargain collectively.
- Established the National Labor Relations Board (NLRB) to enforce labor laws and mediate disputes.
- Long-Term Economic Stabilization

Monetary Policy:

- The Federal Reserve's policies were adjusted to increase the money supply and lower interest rates, stimulating economic growth and investment.
- The U.S. abandoned the gold standard, allowing more flexibility in monetary policy.

Impact and Legacy

- The New Deal programs and reforms helped stabilize the economy, reduce unemployment, and restore confidence in the financial system. While the Great Depression did not fully end until the onset of World War II, which spurred massive economic growth and industrial production, the New Deal laid the foundation for a more robust and resilient economic system.

Challenges and Criticisms
Criticism from Business Leaders and Conservatives:

- Some argued that New Deal policies were too interventionist and stifled free enterprise.

Judicial Challenges:

- Several New Deal programs faced legal challenges, with some being declared unconstitutional by the Supreme Court. This led to adjustments and the creation of new legislation.

Incomplete Recovery:

- Despite significant progress, the economy did not fully recover until the increased production demands of World War II.

Conclusion

- The solutions to the Great Depression, primarily through the New Deal, involved comprehensive and multifaceted approaches to provide immediate relief, promote economic recovery, and implement long-term reforms. These efforts helped to mitigate the effects of the Depression and established a foundation for future economic stability and social welfare programs.

Connection Between the Dust Bowl and the Great Depression

- The Dust Bowl exacerbated the effects of the Great Depression in the affected regions, as farmers who were already struggling due to economic conditions now faced environmental devastation. The combined impact led to widespread migration, and further economic distress, and prompted the government to take action, such as the establishment of the Soil Conservation Service to promote better farming practices and the development of social safety nets and economic reforms under the New Deal.